Class, Elite, and Community in African Development

Alpheus Manghezi

The Scandinavian Institute of African Studies
Uppsala 1976

ISBN 91-7106-099-5
Printed in Sweden by
Bohusläningens AB, Uddevalla 1976

Contents

Preface

In 1964 Alpheus Manghezi, the author of this book—born in South Africa, and in the early sixties employed as a civil servant in Lusaka, Zambia—applied for a scholarship to the Swedish International Development Authority (SIDA) to study sociology in Sweden. SIDA decided that there were equally good opportunities to study this subject at some African universities where, furthermore, sociology might be expected to be taught in a way more relevant to African conditions; and he was given a scholarship to study at the University of Ibadan, Nigeria.

Most of the courses taught in Ibadan at that time represented a structural-functional outlook as expounded in American sociology textbooks and British social anthropology. Myself—at that time professor and head of the department of sociology at the University of Ibadan—wrestled with the limitations of structural functionalism without really having succeeded in anything but adding *ad hoc* revisions concerning structural strain, class and conflict to this theoretical body of Western academic sociology and social anthropology. Whether Alpheus Manghezi could extract any sociological wisdom more relevant to the African context from his courses at Ibadan than he would have done at a Swedish university, I do not know. But I am sure that he learnt a lot simply from being in Nigeria and following the events there from 1965 to 1968.

On my return to Sweden in 1969 I came to realize that one could learn more there about the causes and problems of underdevelopment — at least in a theoretical sense—than in some highly Westernized universities in underdeveloped countries. Of course this is just another manifestation of one of the more recalcitrant features of underdevelopment: the dominance and advance of overseas metropoles at the expense of dependent countries still largely submerged in the colonial heritage.

When Alpheus Manghezi joined me in Uppsala, Sweden, it struck me even more forcefully that a study of the roots of underdevelopment should involve a study not only *of* highly industrialized countries in their historical and contemporary relations to countries in Asia, Africa and Latin America, but also *in* industrialized countries. Not only because a lot of the relevant documents and data are easier to find in this setting but also because opposing theories of development and underdevelopment often are more clearly and seriously articulated and confronted here than in most universities in Africa up till recently.

The present book certainly articulates opposition to the more traditional concepts and approaches of Western sociologists. It does this with an energy and fervour which derives its strength both from a broad-based African experience and a thorough immersion in various aspects of Western thought and reality. But Manghezi is not a neutral observer. His standpoint is clear—and so is the intellect he applies in critically scrutinizing some sociological tracts on elites and community development from the standpoint he is taking.

I have no doubt that his book—lucidly written as it is—can help to bring Africa back to Africans, for instance as a textbook at African universities.

Uppsala in February 1976

Ulf Himmelstrand

Acknowledgments

I wish to express my thanks and gratitude to the Bank of Sweden, Tercentenary Fund, for the generous financial support which has enabled me to pursue my initial research at the Institute of Sociology, University of Uppsala, during the period September 1969 to October 1971.

From the Tercentenary Fund, I also received a grant equal to half of the cost of my return train ticket from London to Peking when I went on a study tour to the People's Republic of China during July and August 1973. This trip, during which I visited several People's Communes and other social institutions, has proved most valuable to me.

Professor Ulf Himmelstrand, Head of the Institute of Sociology, University of Uppsala, whom I have known since 1965 as my teacher and Head of the Department of Sociology at the University of Ibadan, Nigeria, has supervised my studies since I came to the University of Uppsala in September 1969. Professor Ulf Himmelstrand, who was also instrumental to my coming to Uppsala, made it possible for me to eventually complete my doctoral thesis by his patient effort not only at supervising my work, but by persuading me not to give up my academic work, when I felt, as I often did, that my real place was "out there", in the community, where I should get more usefully involved in attempts to solve some of the pressing practical social problems. For all this, and many other ways in which he tried to assist me, I owe him a big debt for which the words "thank you very much" are but an inadequate token of repayment.

I wish to thank Dr. Pablo Suarez, Institute of Sociology at the University of Uppsala, for the trouble he has taken to read my manuscript at its final stages. I have found the critical remarks and comments which he made most valuable.

Various other individuals, friends, and my own family, have given a helping hand towards the completion of my doctoral dissertation. However, only one person remains answerable for this academic effort in all its entirety, and that is me.

Institute of Sociology
University of Uppsala, Sweden.
May 1976.

Alpheus Manghezi

9

I Introduction

Scope of the paper

The paper covers the independent states of tropical Africa (South of the Sahara). Its main focus, however, is on the ex-British rather than the ex-French colonies. This bias is necessitated by two factors—language and familiarity. As I am not literate in the French language, most of the written materials about the former French territories are inaccessible to me. In terms of personal experience, I am much more familiar with conditions in the former British territories, in some of which I have worked and studied for a number of years.[1*]

The thesis of this paper is that the conventional models of social analysis and theories of development are not relevant to the developmental needs of the independent states of tropical Africa and other parts of the underdeveloped world to which they are being exported for use. Furthermore, the thesis is that these theories not only lack relevance, but actually act to perpetuate and intensify the very problems they are supposed to help in solving in the underdeveloped countries.[2]

This being the case, the objectives of radical scholarship in Africa should not only be the exposure of the inherent weaknesses of these theories; radical scholarship must go further and attempt to find more relevant methods for the study and liquidation of the problems of underdevelopment. The struggle against the introduction and perpetuation of these conservative theories in Africa can only be waged successfully by social scientists with a radically different political and ideological orientation, i.e. these scientists have to be *committed*, in contrast to the "un-committed" or "neutral" social scientists who currently dominate African scholarship.

This paper is not based on original field research. However, it is informed and inspired by several years of social work practice, including participation in the training of social workers.[3] This analysis, therefore, consists in the critical examination of some of the available literature on the particular subjects under review. The author hopes, thereby, to contribute in some way to the on going debate about the problems of development and change in tropical Africa.

Chapter I of the paper provides the setting within which the problems of development and change, and the theories and models of development are to be understood.

[1*] Numbered notes will be found at the end of the paper.

Chapters II and III give detailed analysis and critique of some of the theories of modernization and community development, taken as typical examples of liberal models of social analysis and development.

Finally, in Chapter IV, we attempt a critical analysis of the notions of class and élite, and the nature of their relationship with one another. Our thesis is that *class analysis*, but not *élite analysis*, is the appropriate and relevant method for the study of Africa and other parts of the underdeveloped and former colonial territories. However, we remain ready and willing to accept and adopt whatever can *be shown to have scientific value in conservative theories*.

This paper attempts to deal with a variety of concepts and themes of differing degrees of complexities: these include notions of colonialism and imperialist penetration, the process of decolonization, social and class formations, class and class struggle, élite, and social and political mobilization. We are conscious of the fact, therefore, that such an attempt is fraught with dangers and formidable analytical problems.

Generalization

I would like to stress the rather obvious problem implicit in any attempted analysis of such a vast and varied area of study as that which is covered by the present exercise, namely the "independent states of tropical Africa". Lack of appreciation of this important question may result in over-simplified conclusions, or even gross distortion of social reality. I therefore, concur with those who have time and again issued warning in reference to the problem of generalization in the study of Africa. For example, one of the most original writers on African society, Amilcar Cabral, has commented:

Although we are in favour of unity from the Mediterranean to the Cape, we must recognize that there is not 'one Africa'. Historically, economically, and culturally, Africa is not one.[4]

These and other similar observations are valid, whatever stage of African historical development one is considering at a given time—whether in reference to pre-colonial or pre-capitalist Africa in which the process of *unequal development* has been at work, or in reference to both colonial and post-colonial Africa in which capitalist development has and continues to intensify and perpetuate lop-sided development.[5]

Taking full cognisance of these dangers, we proceed to make generalizations in this study because there are over-riding factors which make generalizations justifiable and useful.[6]

All these states of tropical Africa, together with other territories in the rest of Africa, Asia and Latin America, share one crucial, uniting experience, namely the fact that they all have suffered and continue to suffer the effects of colonial and imperialist penetration by the capitalist countries of Western Europe and North America. Through imperialist conquest and subjugation, all these territories were drawn and became fully integrated into the worldwide capitalist system—albeit as dependencies or satellites destinated to fulfil certain historical roles defined for them by the metropolitan powers.[7]

Decolonization

After many years, and in some cases centuries, of colonial rule in tropical Africa, the process of decolonization finally got under way with the granting of independence to the Gold Coast (now Ghana) in 1957. At the time the fact that many of the colonial powers seemed suddenly, as it were, ready and willing to concede political freedom, under what (with the help of hindsight) appeared to be minimal political protest and agitation from the colonial subjects, did not seem particularly incomprehensible.[8]

Why were the imperialist powers suddenly so willing to forego their vested interests which they had guarded with dedication and even sacrifice for centuries? What was the meaning and significance of this process of decolonization, which involved in some cases, forcing independence down the throats of nationalist leaders who said at that stage, that they were not ready for such freedom and were appealing to their departing masters not to abandon them with such undue haste?[9]

This change of *tactics* and not of *strategy,* on the part of the imperialist powers *was necessitated by changed conditions in the international political scene which became more manifest at the end of the Second World War.* Paul Baran has commented about this situation in the following way:

... Weakened by the Second World War, *and no longer able to withstand the pressure for national liberation in the colonies, the imperialist powers were compelled to bow to the inevitable and to grant political independence to those countries in which the anti-imperialist forces were strongest, in which they could not possibly expect to maintain further their colonial rule.* In the words of John Foster Dulles, 'when the fighting in World War II drew to a close, the greatest single political issue was the colonial issue. *If the West had attempted to perpetuate the status quo of colonialism, it would have made violent revolution inevitable and defeat inevitable.* The only policy that might succeed was that of bringing independence peacefully to the more advanced of the 700 dependent persons'.[10] (My emphasis.)

The significance of this passage lies in the fact that it helps us both towards a better understanding of the real meaning of *political freedom* so readily granted by colonial powers, and the role of US imperialism which has either been denied or greatly under-rated. Ruth First clarifies and brings out the content of this passage for us:

Independence was breaking out all over the French empire, and the British; and over the Dutch and the Belgian, as well. There were international reasons why. Already by

1945 the war had fundamentally altered the pre-war structure of power. United States policy was to supplant European imperialism with paternalist and *profitable economic ties*; in place of old-style colonies would be the *new containment*, in United States free enterprise ... For the United States, ... support or opposition to European colonialism would depend on the extent to which their interested European nation respected American global goals elsewhere; and so, most significantly for Africa and Asia and Latin America, on the nature of local political opposition within the colony. If leftwing forces led the independence movement, then the Americans would sustain collaborationists if possible, or a colonial power if necessary. *Decolonization was a move to shore up 'stabilizing' forces in restless regions, rather than a recognition of the right of peoples to the independence and the freedom* that the phrases of the United Nations so eloquently embodied.[11] (My emphasis.)

The extent and degree to which the decolonization strategy advocated by Foster Dulles and others, has succeeded, hardly requires much emphasis: genuine independence has only been achieved by a few countries within the whole range of the underdeveloped countries, while most of the former colonial territories only qualify as neo-colonial or satellite states whose colonial umbilical cords are yet to be severed from the "mother country".[12]

The final act of submission to neo-colonial status offered by the decolonization process could have left no doubt as to the future prospects of the states of tropical Africa, considering the fact, for example, that

When colonial power, on the one hand, for reasons of its own occasionally suggested a variation of its own governmental forms, African politicians protested that they wanted the model intact. So London or Paris or Brussels models were prepared for export; and universities, law courts, local government and the civil service were cut according to the master pattern. The élites of the British territories hankered after the so-called Westminster model.[13]

African Social Research: It has been pointed out by several writers on Africa that before World War II, Western social scientists hardly showed interest in Africa as a fruitful area of social investigation; ethnographers and social anthropologists, usually under the employ of the colonial administration, were the exception. What we wish to point out here is the important fact that the sudden interest shown by Western social scientists on Africa after the War, was largely connected to "Cold War" politics. This factor in the motivation of these social scientists has important bearing and implications for the direction, content and purpose of research in which they engage.

Many liberal social scientists themselves have described these observations even in more apt and eloquent terms than we can hope to equal. The well-known Swedish economist, Gunnar Myrdal, has written, for example:

This tremendous redirection of our work has not been an autonomous and spontaneous development of social science, but a result of vast political changes. Three changes, closely interrelated, stand out sharply: first, the rapid liquidation of the colonial power structure; second, the emergence of a craving for development in the underdeveloped countries themselves, ... and third, the international tensions, culminating in the cold war, that have made the fate of the underdeveloped countries a *matter of foreign policy* in the developed countries. So far as Western countries, scholars and scholarly institutions are concerned, *it is clear that the third cause has been foremost in arousing interest in the problems of the underdeveloped countries.* In the underdeveloped countries themselves it is fairly well understood by their intellectuals—and has occasionally given rise to slightly cynical comments—that the readiness to give aid, and more fundamentally, the interest of both West and the Soviet Union in their conditions and problems were largely due to the world tensions that give significance to their internal affairs.[14] (My emphasis.)

This passage, together with the rest of what has been said in the preceding pages, will provide the necessary background towards a better understanding of the problems of African underdevelopment and the theories of modernization and development which we now proceed to examine.

Notes

1. I have first hand experience of the politics of independence from Zambia and Nigeria. When Zambia became independent in 1964, I had already been in the country, where I was employed as a civil servant, for nearly a year. In this position I was intimately involved in some of the debates as to whether or not the British public administration model should be adopted *intact* or with some *modifications.* I was also involved in the training of social workers as one of the fieldwork student supervisors.
2. Buchanan, Keith, *Reflections on Education in the Third World,* (Bertrand Russel Peace Foundation, Spokesman Books, 1975) p. 12.
3. I have worked as a social worker in Johannesburg, in Glasgow (2 years), in Zambia, and the East End of London.
4. Cabral, Amilcar, *Our People are our Mountains,* (London, Committee for Freedom in Mozambique, Angola and Guinea, 1971) p. 22.
   Hughes, Glyn, "Preconditions for Socialist Development in Africa", in *Socialist Development in Africa* (Africa Research Group, Reprint No. 7, n.d.). Hughes writes on page 11 that:
   > In the last ten years more than thirty African countries South of the Sahara regained political independence from colonial rule. These countries represent a great range of differing economic and political conditions, and any attempt to generalize from their varied experience runs the risk of oversimplification and distortion. However, there are some common factors in their experience—particularly the *acquisition of nominal political independence which left the colonial economic structure largely intact, the external pressures from monopoly capitalism these countries have faced, and the inherent problems of economic underdevelopment*—which make some generalization possible and worthwile. (My emphasis.)
5. The historical studies of Basil Davidson, among others, give excellent descriptions of the varied stages of development reached by different African countries at different epochs. See, for instance, his *The Growth of African Civilization: History of West Africa, 1000—1800* (Longman, Green and Co., 1965).
   Szentes, Tamás, *The Structure of Society and its Changes in the African Countries* (Studies in Developing Countries No. 76, Budapest, 1975). On page 10, the author comments as follows:
   > The distortion of the social structure, the extent of the survival of the pre-capitalist formations, as well as the place and role of these formations in the

social structure naturally vary from one country to another, depending partly on the particular historical period which *originally* produced these remnants, i.e. on the particular stage of historical development at which the intruding foreign capitalism found these societies, and partly on the changes these remnants had to undergo under external effects and fitted into a heterogeneous structure, and how and to what extent they adjusted—viz. pre-colonial—developmental differences, *too*, distorted remnants of a great variety of periods of the primitive communal, slave and feudal societies can be found in the countries of Africa. (Emphasis in the original.)

6. Wilson, Monica, and Thompson, Leonard, *The Oxford History of South Africa*, Vols. I—II (Oxford University Press, 1969 and 1971). This publication seems to mark what might be called a more genuine attempt by South African white liberal scholarship to correct the gross distortion which has so far characterised the analysis of that country's history.

7. Green, Felix, *The Enemy: What Every American Should Know about Imperialism* (Vintage Books, New York, 1971). On page 101, Green states that:

   The substance of imperialism is economic exploitation of other people buttressed by military and political domination. Colonialism is only one method by which such exploitation is achieved. Britain herself learned that it was not always necessary to set up formal colonial rule . . . to reap the benefits.
   There were countries in South America—never part of the British Empire—over which Britain exercised enormous influence through finance and commerce. To-day the US exercises this influence.

8. Because of the success of the decolonization strategy, the necessity for armed struggle was generally averted, except in few instances such as Algeria, in most of the African territories. The intransigence of the remaining colonial powers in Africa, on the other hand, has necessitated a protracted armed struggle, some of which have recently ended with the seizure of political power by the liberation movements in Mozambique, Angola and Guinea-Bissau, former Portuguese colonies.

9. Bello, Ahmadu, *My Life*, (Cambridge University Press, 1962) pp. 118—119.

10. Baran, Paul, A., *The Political Economy of Growth*, (Monthly Review, Modern Paperback edition, New York, 1968) p. 220.

11. First, Ruth, *The Barrel of a Gun: Political Power in Africa and the Coup d'Etat*. (Allen Lane, The Penguin Press, 1970) p. 49.
   Post, Ken, *The New States of West Africa*, (Penguin Books, Harmondsworth, England, 1964). See especially pages 18—19 for the definition of decolonization by a former French Commissioner for the Colonies.
   Jones, G. S., "The History of US Imperialism", in *Ideology and Social Science: Readings in Critical Social Theory*, edited by Robin Blackburn (Fontana/Collins, 1972) pp. 207—37. On page 209, Jones makes the following comments:

   This official interpretation of the background to twentieth century American power has been skilfully elaborated in hundreds of volumes replete with an apparent apparatus of scholarship. For the most part, these legends have taken the form of a knowing or unknowing confusion between imperialism and colonialism. The *invisibility* of American imperialism when compared with the territorial colonialism of European countries, has been internalized by its historians to such an extent, that with a clear conscience they have denied its very existence. Whether this has been the result of State Department gold or simple inability to grasp conceptual distinctions, the end product has been the same: it has meant, in the words of Barrington Moore, astute propaganda but bad history and bad sociology. (Emphasis in the original.)

   Cf. Amin, Samir, *Neo-Colonialism in West Africa* (Penguin Books, Harmondsworth, England, 1973).

16

12. Buchanan, K., op.cit. p. 12. On the same page, Buchanan makes reference to the *need* to liberate the educational system, and this applies equally to the whole socio-economic system of an independent country. He says:

> Vittachi's analysis is concerned chiefly with the new élites of Britain's former colonies in South Asia but the general picture he paints is valid, with appropriate regional nuances, for most of the Third World; only in a handful of countries has an effort been made to strike out along quite different lines and to create an educational system whose objectives and values are more congruent with the needs of Third World societies.

Cf. Woddis, Jack, *Introduction to Neo-Colonialism: The New Imperialism in Asia, Africa and Latin America.* (International Publishers, New York, 1967).

13. First, Ruth, op.cit., p. 51.

14. Myrdal, Gunnar, *Asian Drama: An Inquiry into the Poverty of Nations.* (Allen Lane, The Penguin Press, 1968) p. 8.

Pieris, Ralph, "The Implantation of Sociology in Asia", in *International Social Science Journal, Vol. XXI, No. 3, 1969.* Pieris takes Myrdal's "revelations" further and registers strong objections to this "academic colonialism", complaining that

> The position of social science in Asian countries was not improved by the post-independence entry of academic institutions of non-colonial powers to the Asian scene, amounting to a 'virtual bombardment of massive Western research on the underdeveloped countries in recent times'!

As Asian masses and even Asian scholars are generally believed to draw no benefit from these intellectual activities, then who does? Pieris tells us:

> The president of a leading American university remarked that during Summer,, faculty members of United States universities 'have scattered to the corners of the earth—not to escape, but to learn. And on their return, *like bees from honey flights, the entire university hive is the beneficiary.* (Emphasis in the original) p. 441.

II Theory of Modernization

The theory of modernization, as an export model from Western capitalist countries, became increasingly used in the study of Africa in the wake of the decolonization process. In the following pages I describe, first, some of the main assumptions which underlie this theory; second, I examine attempts made by some of the exponents of this theory to salvage it following severe criticism the model has sustained after its introduction and application to the study of problems of development and change throughout the underdeveloped world, and finally, I shall assess the significance of reforms that have been proposed as a result of this salvage attempt.

Assumptions

The theory of modernization, whether in the field of sociology, social anthropology, political science and so forth, "rests on a supposed dualism between, on the one hand a modern, industrial developed sector and, on the other hand, a traditional, stagnant and underdeveloped sector".[1]

Viewed at an international level, the theory of modernization assumes a dichotomy between one set of countries which are defined as "traditional" and another set viewed as "modern". These two allegedly mutually exclusive societies, are then apportioned certain sets of values or attributes which, in the case of traditional societies are seen in negative terms, i.e. these attributes are not conducive to socio-economic development and change. In respect of the modern societies, however, the attributes which they are said to possess, are seen in positive terms, namely as those which promote development and change. In this way, socio-economic development and change come to be seen by modernization theorists generally, as a process through which a given traditional society moves from a state of "non-modernity" to one which is modern. The American sociologist, Marion J. Levy, sees this process as inevitable:

All these present relatively nonmodernized societies will change in the direction of greater modernization. They will change in that direction regardless of whether their members wish it or whether the members of some other society or societies wish to force such change upon them.[2]

It was another American sociologist, Talcott Parsons, who formulated the most polarized distinction between the attributes of traditional societies on the one hand, and those of modern societies on the other. Parsons has called his indices of "modernity" and "tradition" "Pattern Variables". These have been interpreted by C. S. Whitaker, a political scientist, in the following way:[3]

Figure 1

Context of Action	Tendency of Traditional Society	Tendency of Modern Society
Orientation toward established socio-political institutions, rules, arrangements	Prescription	Innovation
Criteria of role recruitment and allocation	Ascription	Achievement
Criteria of distribution and rewards	Privilige and status	Performance, skill, contribution to objective goals
Quality of official relationships	Diffuse functions, personal loyalty	Specific functions, impersonal loyalty
Sanction of authority	Divine, sacred	Secular
Criteria of membership and participation	Particularistic	Universalistic

When we look more closely at some of these pairs of "pattern variables", we can see how individuals, to whom they are attributed, are supposed to think, act and behave in dealing with their everyday problems:

Prescription vs. innovation: In traditional societies, it is assumed that people will generally act in such a way as to foster or perpetuate conformity based on past experience, and such a behaviour is said to be inimical to social change. In contrast, people in modern societies are assumed generally to behave in ways which facilitate or promote social change, resulting in the general improvement of the objective conditions of their lives.

Ascription vs. achievement: In traditional societies the basis of appointment or recruitment to public office is said to be generally decided on personal consideration, e.g., on the applicant's family or social background, whereas in modern societies such an appointment would, supposedly, be based on the objective abilities of the applicant, i.e. on the person's actual qualifications which can be confirmed objectively, for instance, by academic achievements.

Diffuseness vs. specificity: In traditional societies, official relationships, i.e. duties and behaviour pertaining to an office, are claimed to be generally unclearly defined, whereas duties and functions pertaining to an official position in modern societies are claimed to be clearly defined, circumscribed, and per-

19

formed accordingly. Furthermore, this is supposed to mean that in situations in which duties are defined diffusely, there tends to be no limit as to what the office-holder is expected to perform, whereas in situations in which relations are specific, expectations tend to be clearly stated and specified.

Particularism vs. universalism: Bredemeier and Stephenson define and describe this pair of pattern variables by stating that another

way in which social structures differ is in terms of the kind of morality institutionalized —what we might call the 'morality of principle' on the one hand, or the 'morality of loyalty' on the other. The 'morality of principle' consists of the expectation that one should treat everyone according to the same abstract, general, *universal* principles. The 'morality of loyalty' is the expectation that one should treat people differently, depending on their *particular* relationship to one. Principle morality or universalism, for example, says that if you see your best friend cheating, you should report him to the professor. Loyalty morality or particularism says, 'My country—may she ever be right; but right or wrong, my country!' Universalism says, 'May she ever be right—if she wants my support'.[4] (Emphasis in the original.)

These pattern variables will receive further critical attention later, but first we must trace their historical origins. The structural-functionalist approach in sociology as developed by Talcott Parsons has its roots, according to Whitaker, in the "idealtypes" of

such sociology greats as Maine, Morgan, Weber, Tönnies and Durkheim . . . These scholars have all advanced parallel concepts of dichotomous relationship of principle of behaviour which they believed underlie Western History—status and contract, societas and civitas, traditional and rational authority, Gesellschaft and Gemeinschaft, mechanical and organic solidarity, respectively.[5]

On the basis of such evidence as this, it should not come as any surprise to see the clear tendency in the modernization theorists, to equate "development" or modernization with *Westernization*, leading them as it does, to the conclusion that modernization means the total destruction of all that is "traditional", and its replacement by what is supposed to be "modern". Daniel Lerner, e.g., postulates and claims in his works, that:

Development will come about only when traditional societies are acculturated by the West—through diffusion of knowledge, skills, values, organization, technology and capital —until over time *its society, culture, and personnel become variants of that which has made the North Atlantic Community economically successful.*[6] (My emphasis.)

Criticism

The theory of modernization as briefly outlined above, constitutes what might be called its "first phase", which, as I have already mentioned, has attracted severe criticism by both conservative and radical scholars. In what follows, the differences between bourgeois and radical criticisms of modernization theory will become clearer, and more importantly, we shall thereby come closer to the central problems which the theory of modernization poses before us.

The main criticisms levelled against the theory of modernization by C. S. Whitaker (on the basis of his research in Northern Nigeria) can be summarised briefly as follows:[7]

1. Modernization theory is an inadequate tool of analysis and it has no universal applicability.

2. Whitaker criticises the assumption, implicit in the theory of modernization, that all societies will change inevitably in the only way which will turn them into a variant of Western society in the end. To him, the theory thus "unsoundly rest on a strictly a priori assumption that for all societies there is only one direction of significant change, culminating in the essentials of modern Western society". (1970 p. 3)

3. Whitaker refutes the dichotomization of social patterns or attributes into water-tight compartments—"and thence the attribution to each of the two sets of qualities thus derived to imaginary classes of societies called 'modern' and 'traditional' respectively".

4. Whitaker maintains that ". . . the image of any apparently 'premodern' society is often false or significantly distorted"; and he basis these arguments on empirical cultural and geographical studies of many other scholars.

Whitaker's criticisms of the theory of modernization and the idealtype approach, lead him to the conclusion that

> . . . The notion of modernization has involved the conceptualization of mutually exclusive classes of societies in terms of certain analytical categories, logical constructs, or what Weber called 'ideal-types'—all these being terms for logically alternative principles which the behaviour of people in modern and traditional societies respectively suggests to the mind of an observer. Thus Weber and others all characteristically insist that 'ideal-types' or principles of action they formulated, like all analytical categories or *heuristic devices or logical constructs, are not the same thing as reality itself—i.e. the actual behaviour of the people concerned.* These principles of action supposedly do not, in other words, predict what, in fact, a given people do or will do. Rather, they constitute observations which the mind derives from observing behaviour in an effort to understand its implications.[8] (My emphasis.)

This is a good observation by Whitaker. However, his general attacks on the theory of modernization constitute an example of liberal criticism. He rightly points out that the path of development for a given "traditional" society is not, and should not be restricted to a choice between either total acceptance or total rejection of the modernization model (or its attributes) as presented above, but that there are several alternatives available to choose from. He is right in showing that the structural-functionalist approach is an inadequate method of social analysis, indicating at the same time, as he does, that the theory of modernization has an implicit ethnocentric bias in that it tends to equate development with Westernization. But all these are rather superficial aspects of the modernization theory, and to merely point them out as inherent weaknesses, does not bring us any nearer to the central problem posed by the theory of modernization. The central question in the theory of modernization is its political and ideological role which directly affect various attempts by people of underdeveloped countries to liberate themselves from imperialist domination and exploitation.[9]

Another example of bourgeois criticism of the theory of modernization is offered by Marion Levy. He makes some detailed criticisms, in particular, of Parsons' pattern variables. He is at pains to refute the idea of viewing societies in terms of those supposed to be *completely traditional*, on the one hand, and on the other, those supposed to be *completely modern*. He writes:

The emphasis on science, the levels of specialization, the lack of self-sufficiency, the materialistic orientations, the concerns with predominantly universalistic ethics, objective recruitment, bureaucracy, etc., these taken together are not characteristic of Western society in general, but only of those Western societies which became *relatively modernized*.[10] (My emphasis.)

Furthermore, whether from the viewpoint of technology ("uses of inanimate sources of power" etc.,) or from the viewpoint of social institutions or the consideration of cultural values, attitudes, etc., Levy maintains that "neither of these elements are either totally absent from or exclusively present in any society. He rejects the dichotomous ways societies have been traditionally categorised by social scientists on the grounds that this method was unsatisfactory and sometimes even pejorative.[11]

Levy goes on to suggest that the correct way of categorizing societies in the study of modernization, is to view societies in terms of those which are *relatively non-modern*, on the one hand, and on the other, those which are *relatively modern*. It is quite clear from this that Levy has no quarrels with the fundamentals of the theory of modernization, least of all its implications for the societies to which the model is being exported for use. Levy is concerned with the polarized manner in which the theory of modernization has been conceptualized and formulated, and he tries to correct this by resorting to mere *relativism*.[12]

Gunder Frank is one among radical critiques of the theory of modernization who has given a systematic and devastating assault on the theory in the context of development theory as a whole. It is from this kind of criticism that we begin to comprehend and come to grips with the essentials of the theory of modernization. Most of Frank's criticism of this model are contained in his *Sociology of Development and Underdevelopment of Sociology*. This penetrating analysis is only possible if it is undertaken within an appropriate frame of reference, and this has been provided by Frank in his "metropolis-satellite" model in which the dialectical relations between the Western capitalist countries and the underdeveloped countries have been firmly established.[13] We don't imply, however, that Frank's model is without its own shortcomings (see pp. 29—30 below).

Frank takes, as his point of departure, three modes of analysis which have been provided by the Parsonian school of modernization.[14] Each mode is then subjected to a penetrating analysis and evaluated on the basis of its theoretical adequacy, empiricial validity and policy effectiveness.

I intend only to cite a few examples from Frank's criticisms to illustrate how he effectively refutes and demolishes the whole modernization edifice.

Frank looks at the index or ideal-type approach, for example, and subdivides it into i) pattern variables (Parsons) and ii) the historical stage approach represented by W. W. Rostow. Frank shows that although Rostow's approach seems to differ from Parsons in that Rostow at least takes history more into account, all these variants commonly assume that underdevelopment is an original state which is characterized by indices of tradition,[15] and that therefore, development and change consist in abandoning these characteristics and adopting those of the developed countries. In reference to the assertion that developed nations are characterized, for example, by universalistic rather than particularistic traits, Frank argues and shows that this claim is only normatively true. As a matter of fact, Frank argues,

... the developed countries export particularism to the underdeveloped ones, wrapped in such universalistic slogans as freedom, democracy, justice, the common good, the economic liberalism of free trade, the political liberalism of free elections, the social liberalism of free social mobility, and the cultural liberalism, of free flow of ideas such as the ones we are examining here.[61]

The second example I wish to cite from Frank's criticisms of modernization theory is that which concerns the dichotomy between role specificity and role diffuseness. In this respect Frank starts by questioning the relevance of the dichotomy itself. He goes on to argue and show that there is really not much point in stressing role specificity and diffuseness, when reality (including American reality—the major source of these theories) frequently show that ". . . the socially significant and dominant roles are collected together in one or a few individuals who wear many hats simultaneously or in quick and institutionalized succession".[17]

Through his penetrating analysis, in which indisputable evidence is marshalled to support arguments, Frank arrives at the conclusion that the modernization model of development must be rejected since from the point of view of the underdeveloped countries all evidence demonstrate that this method is theoretically inadequate, empirically invalid and ineffective policy-wise. The theory of modernization therefore, cannot be expected to contribute to a proper understanding and eradication of the problems of underdevelopment. On the contrary, the theory of modernization contributes significantly to the perpetuation of these problems throughout the underdeveloped nations. By ignoring the historical and structural realities of the underdeveloped countries, modernization theorists attempt to conceal the root cause of the very problems they claim to be intent on solving. The real purpose of the modernization approach is revealed in a passage quoted by Frank from one of Parson's followers:

Marx, however, tended to treat the socio-economic structure of capitalist enterprise as a single indivisible entity rather than breaking it down analytically into a set of distinct variables involved in it. It is this analytical breakdown which is for present purpose the most distinctive feature of modern sociological analysis... It results in the modification of the Marxian view ... *The primary structural emphasis no longer falls on ... the theory of exploitation but rather on the structure of occupational roles.*[18] (My emphasis.)

Frank goes on to show that this expressed purpose or use of modernization theory does not originate in the present works of Parsons and others, but can be traced to the classical works of the pioneers, of the "ideal-type" approach:

Being a true holist, Marx was led inevitably, as Parsons (has) pointed out, ... to the observation that exploitation is a necessary basis of this system and to the conclusion that such a basis generates the polarization of the system. Since this conclusion was not palatable to Social Democrats such as Weber and Durkheim, whose disciple Parsons became, they set out to construct an alternative theory of the social system by starting with its parts rather than with the whole—a procedure which, as Parsons says, inevitably de-emphasizes exploitation.[19]

The political and ideological roles of the theory of modernization as an export model for use in underdeveloped countries, is spelled out in no uncertain terms by none other than Talcott Parsons in his *Structure and Process in Modern Societies,* in the special section devoted to the analysis of "The Problems of Underdeveloped Areas."[20]

The first point to note here is Parsons' ahistorical treatment of the ex-colonial territories. He mentions the colonial past which links these countries to the capitalist system only in passing, and in so doing he also tries to minimize the role of United States imperialism. Secondly, as we have seen in connection with his pattern variables, development for these ex-colonial territories lies in the general direction leading to a Western type of society.

Although the actual problems of the underdeveloped countries are not discussed in any meaningful way, Parsons sees a definite and decisive role that Western countries, especially the United States, must play in "helping" these countries solve their problems. These problems, in which Western countries must pay particular attention, are in the provision of educational or training facilities and the creation of political *stability.*[21]

In reference to education and training, Parsons warns that it is important for Western countries, first to make a careful selection of which social groups they are going to support in a given country (see page 13 above). It is most important that such a choice must not, inadvertently, results in strengthening the hand of the communists at the expense of Western interests. Once the correct choices have been made, Parsons counsells, then the next practical step should be

... The building-up, under the 'umbrella' of government, of a strong highly educated and —in the requisite proportions and fields—technically trained class of people whose primary social status is bound-up with occupational careers of the modern type and who thus come to be dissociated from any traditional élite groups in their society. It must in some sense be a functional equivalent of the Western 'middle class.'[22]

24

In regard to the political question, it should be noted that although Parsons hardly pays attention to historical factors, he is not entirely blind of these factors and their significance. He is aware, for example, to the fact that

The political and social agencies of a recently emancipated ex-colonial world makes for great haste in development. Because of this and the inherited antagonism to colonialism, it is unlikely that private enterprise on the nineteenth century model can have much prospect of spreading widely, very soon. Governments, acting in the name of 'nationalism' and 'socialism', are likely to be by far the most important agencies.[23]

In Parsons' view, the threat to political stability in the newly independent states is posed by the probability of a communist takeover.[24] Looking at the states of tropical Africa today, Parsons would be hard-put to point out from among the several army takeovers, any which constitutes a "communist takeover".

Rounding up his proposed political and ideological strategies through which Western countries can maintain and perpetuate their imperialist domination and exploitation of the underdeveloped countries in the post-colonial era, Parsons concludes that

The main alternative for the time being is a development in the direction of 'democratic socialism', in which intellectuals who have an important contact with Western culture are bound to play a prominent role.[25] (My emphasis.)

What the foregoing analysis has shown is that, having no scientific use towards a comprehension of the problems of socio-economic development and change and their eradication in the underdeveloped countries, the theory of modernization, has political, ideological and propaganda uses which pose enormous problems for national liberation from imperialist domination.

To the rescue

What was to become of the model of modernization after it had sustained these severe blows which left it in ruins, and with the radical critics calling for no less than its complete rejection?

In this *Tradition, Change, and Modernity*, S. N. Eisenstadt has made attempts to salvage and reformulate the model of modernization.[26] That Eisenstadt has undertaken this arduous task is not surprising when it is remembered that he is one of those who have contributed substantially to the original formulations and articulation of the theory of modernization.

Eisenstadt describes his own effort at an attempted reform of the theory of modernization as a "shift" which is to be seen in the context of major shifts that "have been taking place in the social sciences, sociology, political science, and anthropology in general and in relation to the study of modernization and development in particular for the last ten to fifteen years". (p. vi.)

In this three hundred page volume, which includes some of his earlier papers on the subject, Eisenstadt describes in great detail, the historical development of the theory of modernization from the perspective of sociology, political science, economics and so forth. Included also, is an analysis of traditional and modern societies from the perspective of classical sociology. After an exhaustive examination of the various criticisms which have been levelled against the theory of modernization, Eisenstadt comes to the conclusion that despite its inherent weaknesses which have been exposed, the theory of modernization should not be discarded, as some have demanded, but should be reformulated and put to use.

On first sight, it is not easy to assess the extent to which Eisenstadt has shifted, and consequently, the significance of that shift, from his previous position on the subject.[27] In view of this problem, I came to the conclusion that the best way toward an assessment of his shift would be through an examination of some of the main criticisms which have been directed at Eisenstadt himself on the basis of his previous work on modernization theory, and then try to see to what extent his present work reflects any significant response that could be seen as constituting a *substantive shift*.

The Dutch sociologist, W. F. Wertheim, has made some severe criticisms of Eisenstadt's earlier works, of which the main ones can be summarised as follows:[28]

1. Wertheim maintains that Eisenstadt fails to take into account in his analysis, the historical relationships that have been forged between the Western capitalist countries and today's underdeveloped nations. Wertheim argues that this constitutes a serious omission which leads Eisenstadt to a position in which he comes to view the cause of underdevelopment almost exclusively in terms of intrinsic factors.

There is no noticeable shift from this position on the part of Eisenstadt. In this present work, Eisenstadt describes colonialism and imperialism euphemistically as "foreign impingement", and positively as the "modernizing impact or influence", while he blames traditional societies for their alleged negative responses to this external influence.[29] According to Eisenstadt, the so-called modernizing influence, comes, as it were, to present to a given traditional society, modern institutional frameworks whose acceptance would enable that country to make a successful "take off" to modernization.

Although Eisenstadt does not seem to hold the view that a given traditional society has either to accept or reject modernization when it is offered, he nevertheless shows his preference in a clear way, for those countries, like India, Turkey and Mexico, which he sees as perfect examples of traditional countries which have positively accepted and adapted themselves to modernization. In contrast, traditional societies, like Imperial China, Indonesia, Burma and Sudan, are cited as examples either of total failure to adapt to modernization, or, at best, as examples of *only partial acceptance of Western influence*. Here again, Eisenstadt places the blame for failure to adapt solely on the structure of traditional society. He does this without betraying a thought that the so-called modernizing agent itself, could in fact act as the obstacle to the emergence of modernizing institutions *from within* the society, or the acceptance of modernizing influence from external sources.[30]

2. Wertheim has accused Eisenstadt of tendencies to viewing political protest and activity, including various popular demands from the masses, largely in negative terms as *disturbances, conflicts* and *social disorganization* whose objectives can only be the general *disruption of established institutions, rules,* etc. Wertheim recognizes the fact that where the "old-timer societies" are concerned, Eisenstadt concedes to the possibility that these political protests might, in certain cases, have made a constructive contribution to the nation's historical development and progress.[31] Nevertheless, Wertheim complains that Eisenstadt has not made any similar concession in the case of mass protests and political unrest in underdeveloped countries.

Wertheim suggests that because of his biased views on mass political action, Eisenstadt, it would appear, "... does not realize that violent eruptions represent a different but equally elementary, and under certain circumstances, inevitable, type of modernization—necessitated by a too high degree of adaptation, amounting to stagnation, or even involution, and of integration which is nothing more than an underdeveloped equilibrium".[32]

Eisenstadt has not made any shift from this position. This position, however, seems to take the form of an ambiguity on the part of Eisenstadt. In his present work this is revealed in his description of some of the achievements of the Chinese Communist Party leadership when he writes:

The specific characteristic of this phase of China's response to the impact of modernity does not lie, of course, in the mere existence of a Communist movement—which can be found in most Asian countries—but in the characteristics of this movement. Most important among these are, first, the ability of the Chinese Communist movement to forge out relatively cohesive leaderships and cadres, and, second, *the ability of this leadership to seize power and attempt (at least with degrees of success as yet very difficult to estimate) to forge a very strong center capable of reestablishing a new, revolutionary, yet seemingly viable (at least in its first phases) social order.*[33] (My emphasis.)

Working, as he does, within the functionalist model of social analysis, Eisenstadt's present work is characterized by an overwhelming emphasis on *integration, adaption,* and the establishment of *institutional frameworks* for the expressed purposes of *absorbing changes* and providing *opportunities* for the *containment* of discontent. Eisenstadt tells us, for example, that "In the political sphere, modernization is characterized first, by the development of a highly differentiated political structure, in terms of specific political roles and institutions, ... of the development of specific political goals and orientations, (and) ... second, political modernization is characterized by a growing extension of the scope of the central legal, administrative, and political activities and their permeation into all spheres and regions of the society, (and) ... third, it is characterized by the continuous spread of potential political power to the wider groups in society —ultimately to all the citizens."[34]

27

This political system is none other than that which has been described so well by Mannheim and Schumpeter (see pp. 70—71 below), incidentally, under similar circumstances when, they too, were making concerted attempts to salvage yet another model. In this political system, the masses are allowed no more than symbolic participation because in this system it is an élite that rules—the so-called modernizing élite whose role in the modernization process is given prominence by Eisenstadt in his present work. (1973 pp. 32—39 and 335—339.)

Betraying the ethnocentricism of which he had earlier been accused, Eisenstadt reveals more clearly how the masses are supposed to participate in this political system:

The culmination of this process (political modernization), as it has *gradually developed in the outright modern systems,* is the participation of the ruled in the *selection* of the rulers, in the setting of the major political goals, and to *a smaller extent in the formulation of policies.* The formal expression of this process is the system of elections, as it has evolved, in different ways, in most modern political systems.[35] (My emphasis.)

3. The third main criticism against Eisenstadt is, according to Wertheim, the former's total commitment to the "ideal-type" model. This accussation is made in the context of the notion of *sustained and continuous modernization without breakdowns* in the field of economic growth, advanced by Eisenstadt. Wertheim argues that by defining the process of modernization in terms of an alleged self-sustaining growth, Eisenstadt reveals himself to be "arguing from a preponderantly Western societal model". As a result of this, Wertheim shows, developmental efforts by the underdeveloped countries come to be seen by Eisenstadt, largely as an attempt to "catch up" with the Western countries. And in all this, Wertheim goes on, "Eisenstadt does not mention the possibility of the backward society overtaking the industrialized states by adopting drastic measures which the latter are unwilling to introduce".[36]

Eisenstadt maintains this original position in his present analysis. And his views in this respect are not diminished even when Eisenstadt resorts to relativism, as he often does. He writes, for example, that ". . . the historically initial cases of modernization (those of Western Europe and the United States) have tended to exhibit *a more or less continuous expansion of indices of social mobilization* together with increasing structural specialization and the *institutional capacity for sustained growth"*.[37] (My emphasis.) This assertion is further supported by Eisenstadt himself who states in his closing remarks that

In the preceding analysis of the European, Indian and Chinese historical experience, we have encountered each of these modes of attitudes to change. Chinese society has been characterized by a continuous oscillation between a negative attitude and a strong traditionality, on the one hand, and a more coercive type of semi-innovative attitude on the other. India has been characterized by a relatively high degree of adaptiveness in its attitude, and European history was marked by a predominance of adaptive and transformative attitudes. Among other societies, the Russian is characterized by coercion and innovation, and the patrimonial societies are usually characterized by a high degree of relatively passive, negative, or limited adaptive attitudes.[38]

From our own examination of the theory of modernization in general, and Eisenstadt's attempts to retrieve the model from the fatal blows it has sustained in its evolution, we come to the conclusion that Eisenstadt has failed in his efforts to salvage the model. The reasons for his failure are not difficult to see, since we have repeatedly pointed them out throughout the foregoing pages:

With his commitment to the Structural-functionalist model, it is inconseivable that Eisenstadt could have effected any significant modification to the theory of modernization while he left the parent-model untouched. And with his hands effectively tied down, as it were, Eisenstadt's promised substantative shift could only amount to a mere tinkering about with the rough edges of the theory of modernization so as to make it appear more credible than in the past. His plea for the reformulation of the relationship between tradition and modernity, intended to avoid the problem of making "traditional societies" and "modern societies" appear as if they were mutually exclusive, has already been made, as we have seen, by other writers such as Whitaker and Levy.[39] In short, Eisenstadt's entire effort to reform the theory of modernization has, as its main result, the *restatement* and *reaffirmation* of the alleged usefulness of the theory of modernization in particular, and the structural-functionalist model in general.

This "shift of emphasis" therefore, constitutes what we termed above, change of tactics rather than of strategy, so as to enable the model to be more efficient in its *absorption* of criticism, to be more *adaptive* to the changing international conditions, and to become more effectively *institutionalized* (if we can borrow from Eisenstadt's own favourite terminology).[40]

In reference to the future prospects for modernization theory, we can do no better than conceding the final word to Eisenstadt:

The preceding analysis, of course, does not aim to imply that the study of indices of mobilization is unimportant or irrelevant to the analysis of the processes of modernization ... The indices are especially important as indicators of what may be called the breaking down or "passing" of premodern society and the disintegration of more closed, traditional and relatively autarchic units ... *Hence, our analysis calls mainly for continuous work in the refinement of the construction of such indices so as to enable one to use them as more sensitive indicators of the direction and crystallization of the process of modernization.*[41] (My emphasis.)

Theory of Dualism: A Note

As the theory of dualism is a branch of the theories of modernization which have just been described in some detail above, no detailed or elaborate discussion of dualism is intended here.[42] But in view of the fact that dualism has often been presented as an independent theory in its own right, we must also give it a special mentioning.

The dual-economy dual-society thesis has often been advanced with its "twin-sibling"—the theory of feudalism, and together have been held by their protagonists as the main barriers or obstacles to socio-economic development and change in the underdeveloped countries.

These theories have received their severest criticism, and deservedly so, from several social scientists. Foremost among these are Gunder Frank, who bases his criticism on his studies of some Latin American countries, and from the South African sociologist, Archie Mafeje, who recently tested the validity of the notion of dualism against the socio-economic reality of South Africa, Rhodesia and the independent states of East and Central Africa.[43]

As it has already been pointed out in the foregoing pages, the notion of dualism, like the theory of modernization, assumes a dichotomy between, on the one hand, a traditional society, and on the other, a modern one. This dichotomy implies that the two sets of societies so identified are almost diametrically opposed in their characteristics. Frank states, for instance, that those who subscribe to this thesis (bourgeois and Marxist analysts alike),

... maintain that the society consists of two substantially independent sectors. The one is modern because it took off more or less independently and is capitalist; and the other, the agrarian sector, *still holds back its own progress and that of the modern sector because it remains feudal.*[44] (My emphasis.)

From his critical studies of Latin America, Frank comes to the conclusion that the assertion of the existence of dualism and feudalism in Latin America (and other parts of the world) is completely unfounded. Frank warns that serious mistakes are going to be made in any effort at finding effective remedies against the problems of underdevelopment if such attempts are based on the erroneous acceptance of the existence of dualism and feudalism. Frank claims that in fact such mistakes have been made in Latin America, where the protagonists of these theories have been calling for the destruction of feudalism as a precondition for development and change in Latin America, when, in Frank's view, the real enemy that must be destroyed is the capitalist system. And, as in the case of the theories of modernization and development, Frank is uncompromising in calling for the total rejection of the notions of dualism and feudalism.[45]

Although Frank's analysis of dualism and feudalism has attracted a great deal of attention, both positive and negative, there is hardly any serious disagreement with his views on dualism as such. However, Frank's analysis has been challenged, and correctly too, for placing too much emphasis on market relations at *the expense of an analysis* of *class relations*, especially of the *internal social structure*. This is a fair criticism of Frank's work, including his "metropolitan-satellite" model, which suffers equally from this serious weakness.[46]

This is a serious weakness in Frank's analysis because failure to recognize and deal appropriately with the role played by internal factors in the process of underdevelopment, will make it very difficult, if not impossible, to device and formulate more appropriate and effective policy measures for the *eradication* of the problems with which the underdeveloped countries are beset. Mafeje has summed up this fundamental question in the following way:

... our unit of analysis is the national *socio-economic system* and the inter\
both as the internal and external moments of the same dialectic or contr\
proper allocation of instances, it is well to remember that from the point of\
developed countries the international system is historically and analytically\
cedurally and strategically ultimate, i.e. for the comprehension of underdev\
dynamic process, it is necessary to understand the former; but for its *liqui*\
grasp of the internal system is indispensable.[47] (Emphasis in the original.)

Mafeje arrives at this conclusions after a closely argued paper in which he produces indisputable evidence on which he basis his total rejection of the theory of dualism.[48]

In support of his arguments, Mafeje shows, among other things, how in the case of South Africa and Rhodesia, the colonial regimes have systemically dispossessed the Africans of their land after the initial military conquests: this land alienation was achieved through various mechanisms including different forms of taxation and legislative and Land Acts. The same mechanisms, adjusted to local conditions, were used in the territories of East and Central Africa; but the end result in all these countries, was of course, the same, namely the artificial creation of the so-called dual economies or dual societies by colonial rule.[49]

When we take a closer look at the way the assertions of the existence of dualism in Africa have been presented by exponents of this theory, we are struck by the apparent absurdity of their arguments. One example will suffice to illustrate this point. Professor William Barber, in his book, *The Economy of British Central Africa: A Study of Economic Development in a Dualistic Society*, has written:

The dualism of society in Rhodesia and Nyasaland is all pervasive phenomenon. It is expressed in all facets of social, political and economic life. But its economic aspects can best be viewed through the contrasting forms of economic organization which co-exist there. At one pole is the money economy organized, financed, and administered largely by Europeans, and heavily dependent on external trade and investment. It functions with money as a medium of exchange and its superficial properties resemble those of more advanced economies. At the opposite end of the spectrum is the traditional economy of the indigenous peoples. Within it, techniques of production are still primitive, productivity is low, and standards of real income often fail to rise much above the minimum required for subsistence.[50]

When Barber proceeds to identify the main characteristics of this region, which includes Zambia (then Northern Rhodesia), as Walter Elkan shows, Barber also succeeds in demonstrating the thesis that rather than being an original state of affairs, dualism is an artificial creation. It is a notion which imperialism attempts to use as a *justification for economic exploitation and political domination of the societies of these regions.* All this is clearly revealed in the following passage in which Barber describes:

How European dominance came into being; how best farm land came to be reserved for European use; and how at times, when the interest of the Africans and Europeans clashed, those of the Europeans were allowed to prevail. Africans were to provide manpower for an expanding economy from which incidental benefits were expected to accrue, but the ob-

...t of an expanding economy was to afford Europeans a comfortable way of life, and to provide opportunities for continued European immigration from Britain and South Africa.[51]

Barber clearly understands the extent and significance of this land alienation as can be seen in the following long passage in which he takes us to the source of dualism, namely practical colonial policy:

The allocation of land in Central Africa has been one of the most powerful reinforcements of this policy. In the Rhodesias, lands most suitable for commercial use have been reserved for Europeans. The dimensions of this problem loom largest in Southern Rhodesia. Of the total area of the colony, roughly half is assigned to Europeans, *predominantly in the fertile High Veld*. Approximately 42 per cent. of Southern Rhodesia is for African use. The bulk of the indigenous population, however, has been compressed into Native Reserves comprising about 22 per cent. of the total acreage. Native Purchase Areas, where Africans of demonstrated agricultural ability may acquire rights of individual tenure, account for another 8 per cent. The allocation and use of this land is regulated by the government and, as yet, much of it remains unoccupied. The remainder of the African area is designated as 'Special Native Areas'. This category of land allocation, created in 1950, has expanded the total acreage available to Africans largely by reducing the area previously unassigned to either race. *As the Special Native Areas include much of the arid and tsetse-infested zone, their African population is light. Of the total African area, much is officially classified as waste land and only about 15 per cent. is regarded as suitable for cultivation.*[52] (My emphasis.)

Why then, in the face of all this evidence, provided by exponents of the theory of dualism themselves, do these social scientists continue and persist in presenting dualism as if it was an original state to be eradicated by the diffusion of capitalist values? We can only conclude that this myopia on the part of these social scientists, is a genuine reflection of their political, ideological and intellectual orientation and commitment. Whether or not this persistence is conscious or unconscious, is, to my mind, quite beside the point.

Notes

1. Marcussen, Henrik, S., "The Theory of Modernization and the Notion of Dualism", in *Dualism and Rural Development in East Africa*, (Institute for Development Research, Denmark, 1973), p. 19.
2. Levy, Marion, J., (Jr)., *Modernization and the Structure of Societies*, Vol. 1 (Princeton University Press, 1966) p. 31.
3. Whitaker, C. S., (Jr)., *The Politics of Tradition: Continuity and Change in Northern Nigeria, 1946—1966* (Princeton University Press, 1970) pp. 8—9.
   Parsons, Talcott, and Shils, Edward, A, *Towards a General Theory of Action*, edited. (Harvard University Press, 1951). On page 82, Parsons discusses his pattern variables under three aspects, namely the *cultural, personality*, and *social system* aspects. However, what is stressed is the *individual or psychological* aspect, by which individuals supposedly perceive reality and act and behave under given conditions. It is largely for this reason that we have chosen Whitaker's analysis of the pattern variables as illustration since the latter's approach is *more sociological*.

Parsons, Talcott., *The Social System*, (Glencoe, Ill, 1957). On page 67, Parsons arranges his "pattern variables" or value orientations in the following way:

    I. The Gratification-Discipline Dilemma: Affectivity vs Neutrality.

    II. The Private vs Collectivity Interest Dilemma: Self-orientation vs Collectivity Orientation.

    III. The choice between Types of value-orientation standard: Universalism vs Particularism.

    IV. The choice between 'Modalities' of the social object: Achievement vs Ascription.

    V. The definition of Scope of interest in the object: Specificity vs Diffuseness.

4. Bredemeier, H. C., and Stephenson, R. M., *The Analysis of Social Systems*, (Holt, Rhinehart and Winston, Inc., 1962) p. 17.

The definition and description of the pattern variables by Bredemeier and Stephenson are more *practical* and *concrete*, and therefore their approach is more preferable than that of Parsons whose definitions and descriptions are largely *metaphysical* and *abstract*. (See, for example, page 82 of *Towards a General Theory of Action*; footnote 3 above.)

5. Whitaker, C. S., op.cit., p. 4.

6. Quoted in Gunder Frank's *Sociology of Development and Underdevelopment of Sociology*, (Zenit Reprint 1, Stockholm, 1969) p. 2.

The Studies of Lerner, e.g., *The Passing of Traditional Society: Modernizing the Middle East*, (New York, 1958), are an example of the acculturation-diffusionist approach.

7. Whitaker, C. S., op.cit., pp. 3—11.

8. Ibid., op.cit., p. 4. Although the problems of colonialism are mentioned in passing, Whitaker devotes his attention to the discrediting of the dichotomous definition of societies into traditional and modern ones. He suggests that in place of *traditional society*, the term "*confrontation society*" should be used, and proceeds to defend its application as follows:

> To reiterate, 'Confrontation society' is a term I have employed to help conceptualize situations in which aspects of institutions of different historical origins actually coexist and interact. It emphatically does not constitute a reappearance in a new guise of the popular concepts and evolutionary assumptions of the older scholarly tradition just discussed. On the contrary, it represents a rejection of them in favour of a perspective which remains open to the possibility that institutions of radically different origin, form and function may be difficult or impossible to accommodate mutually in some important respects but not in others. (pp. 11—14).

9. See Chapter III.

10. Levy, M. J., op.cit., p. 90.

11. Ibid., op.cit., pp. 85—92.

12. Ibid., op.cit., pp. 9—15. Marion Levy denies that ideology and imperialism are central questions posed by the theory of modernization (see pp. 16 and 85). His outright denial comes out more clearly when he argues, on page 125 (vol. 1) that:

> The problems of modernization for late-comers have almost uniformly been discussed in the context of imperialism. It so happens that all the initial cases were in fact carried out under the spur of this particular sort of interference, *but emphasis on this form of interference has grossly obscured the problems involved.* Like most people today, I happen to detest imperialism as it has existed and have no desire to deny its evils. I do wish, however, *to point out that the morals of imperialists are essentially irrelevant to the problems faced by members of relatively nonmodernized societies in contact with modernization.* (My emphasis.)

13. Frank, Andre, Gunder, *Sociology of Development and Underdevelopment of Sociology* (Zenit Reprint 1, Stockholm, 1969). The "metropolis-satellite" model is described in several of Frank's books, including a well articulated article, "The Development of Underdevelopment", in *Monthly Review, Vol. 18, No. 4, 1966.*

14. Ibid., op.cit., pp. 1—3—The three modes are, the index or ideal-type mode; the acculturation mode; and the so-called "process analysis mode" of studying underdeveloped countries.

15. Ibid., op.cit., p. 4.
   On page 18, Frank makes the following comments:
   > Rostow's stages and thesis are incorrect primarily because they do not correspond at all to the past or present reality of the underdeveloped countries whose development they are supposed to guide. It is explicit in Rostow that underdevelopment is the original stage of what are supposedly traditional societies—that there are no stages prior to the present stage of underdevelopment. It is further explicit in Rostow that the now developed societies were once underdeveloped. But all this is quite contrary to fact. This entire approach to economic development and cultural change attributes history to the developed countries but denies all history to the underdeveloped ones.

16. Ibid., op.cit., p. 5.
   Robinson, Joan, *Freedom and Necessity: An Introduction to the Study of Society,* (George Allen and Unwin, London, 1970). Dealing with the *particularism* of "free trade", Robinson points out on page 106 that:
   > Every nationalist or reformist political party in the Third World is labelled 'communist' and kept out of power, by force if necessary, so that these regimes (with one or two precarious exceptions), willingly or reluctantly, *keep their economies open to trade and investment, for the convenience of capitalist business* and, in many cases, put their territory and their forces at the disposal of US strategy...
   > *The obligation to remain within the rules of the game of the world market puts a number of obstacles in the way of development...* It is against the rules to expropriate landlords and make use of rent. The profits of native industry are largely consumed in supporting a middle class standard of life. A great deal of the profits generated by exploiting the natural resources of these countries accrues to foreign business, etc., ... (My emphasis.)

17. Frank, A. G., op.cit., p. 7. Frank, however, accepts the partial correctness of the dichotomy between role specifity and role diffuseness, as he says on page 10:
   > Finally, Hoselitz says that roles in underdeveloped countries are funtionally diffused rather than specific. This is true in part. The poor in the underdeveloped countries, whether classified as working in the primary, secondary, or tertiary sector, do indeed practice many professions at a time, such as farmer, trader, peddler, artisan, odd jobber, thief and provider of social security to others, in an attempt to keep body and soul together.

18. Ibid., op.cit., p. 14.
   Lenin, V. I., *Selected Works,* (Progress Publishers, Moscow, 1971). Lenin has issued a serious warning to us to be on the guard against repreated attempts by both bourgeois and vulgar Marxist writers to emasculate the Marxist revolutionary theory. He writes, on page 266:
   > What is now happening to Marx's theory has, in the course of history, happened repeatedly to the theories of revolutionary thinkers and leaders of oppressed classes fighting for emancipation. During the life time of great revolutionaries, the oppressing classes constantly hounded them, received their theories with the most savage malice, the most furious hatred and the most unscrupulous campaigns of lies and slander. After their death, attempts are made to convert them into

harmless icons, to canonise them, so to say, and to hallow their *names* to a certain extent for the 'consolation' of the oppressed classes and with the object of duping the latter, while at the same time robbing the revolutionary theory of its *substance*, blunting its revolutionary edge and vulgarizing it. Today, the bourgeoisie and the opportunists within the labour movement concur in this doctoring of Marxism. They omit, obscure, or distort the revolutionary side of this theory, its revolutionary soul. They push to the foreground and extol what is or seems acceptable to the bourgeoisie.

19. Ibid., op.cit., p. 45.
20. Parsons, Talcott, *Structure and Process in Modern Societies,* (Glencoe, Ill. 1960) pp. 116—131.
21. Ibid., op. cit., pp. 124—125.
22. Ibid., op.cit., p. 127. This refers specifically to the training of staff to man "specialized bureaucratic organizations".
23. Ibid., op.cit., p. 129.
24. Ibid., op.cit., p. 127.
25. Ibid., op.cit., p. 129.
    Worsley, Peter, *The Third World,* (Weidenfeld and Nicolson, London, 1964). An example of this opportunistic "radicalism", a posture advocated by Parsons, is shown by Worsley (p. 135) when he tells us that:

    > In a few territories such as the Ivory Coast, relatively prosperous and differentiated, the prosperous farmer was dominant in the leadership. Its characteristic spokesman was Houghouet Boigny. *But though the son of a wealthy planter, and a chief and a large planter himself,* he led the great mass party of French West Africa, the Ressemblement Democratique Africaine, *into alliance with the French Communist Party...* But the attraction of the Communist Party was its militancy, not its communism. The more bourgeoisified élites, once they have gained political control, quickly lose their radicalism, especially in the more prosperous territories. And after his flirtation with the PCF, Houghouet Boigny settled down to a more congenial role as a *pillar of the French establishment.* Before long, he was Minister in the Cabinet that planned Suez. (My emphasis.)

    The *class character* of this opportunism is further confirmed and demonstrated today by Houghouet Boigny's open collaboration with the South African white minority regime's so-called policy of detente—a *counter revolutionary offensive aimed at the containment and destruction of the radical liberation movements in Southern Africa.*
26. Eisenstadt, S. N., *Tradition, Change and Modernity* (John Wiley and Sons, Inc., 1973).
27. Ibid., op.cit. Eisenstadt patiently and meticulously describes the emergence and development of the theories of modernization from the perspectives of different social sciences, including most of his earlier papers on the subject, in the most "objective" and "neutral" manner.
28. Wertheim, W. F., *Evolution and Revolution: Rising Waves of Emancipation,* (Penguin Books, Harmondsworth, England, 1974) pp. 78—85.
    Eisenstadt's book which is the direct focus of Wertheim's criticisms is *Modernization, Protest and Change* (Englewood, Cliffs, New Jersey, Prentice Hall, 1966).
29. Eisenstadt, S. N., op.cit., p. 265.
30. Ibid., op.cit., see pp. 40, 47, and especially pp. 261—305.
31. Wertheim, W. F., op.cit., p. 81.
32. Ibid., op.cit., p. 84.
33. Eisenstadt, S. N., op.cit., p. 276.
34. Ibid., op.cit., p. 24.
35. Ibid., op.cit., p. 24.
36. Wertheim, W. F., op.cit., p. 79. On the same page, Wertheim adds that:

Moreover, in Eisenstadt's theory, the chances that the sudden spurt will be successful are rather slight. The initial backwardness remains in his analysis a serious disadvantage throughout the modernization process. The odds are that the development will be hampered by serious tensions or eruptions, and even breakdowns are far from unlikely.

37. Eisenstadt, S. N., op.cit., p. 28.
38. Ibid., op.cit.. pp. 329—330.
39. Ibid., op.cit., p. 262.
   Marcussen, H. S., op.cit. This author gives an excellent summary of the inherent weaknesses of theories of modernization on page 19.
40. Beginning with the October 1917 Revolution in Russia, several socialist states and revolutionary political movements have emerged and continue to develop and make their impact and influence felt throughout the world. At the same time, in the academic field, radical and revolutionary scholarship has been growing rapidly. It is all these historical events which explain the various "shifts" in the general strategy of imperialism and liberal scholarship.
41. Eisenstadt, S. N., op.cit., pp. 30—31.
42. Szentes, Tamás, *The Political Economy of Underdevelopment*, (Akadémiai Kiadó, Budapest, 1971).
   Szentes suggests that "As an independent theory, it (Dualism) appears in two main variants (a) the theory of *sociological dualism* and (b) the theory of *technological dualism*", (p. 74) (emphasis in the original). For the *psychological aspects* of dualism, see the passage quoted from Lucien Pye's book, page 106 below, footnote 40.
43. Frank, A. G., *Capitalism and Underdevelopment in Latin America: Historical Studies of Chile and Brazil,* (Monthly Review Press Modern Reader Paperback Edition, 1969).
   Mafeje, Archie, "The Fallacy of Dual Economies Revisited", in *Dualism and Rural Development in East Africa,* (Institute for Development Research, Denmark, 1973) pp. 27—51.
44. Frank, A. G., *Capitalism and Underdevelopment in Latin America . . .*, op.cit., p. 238.
   Suyin, Han, *China in the Year 2001,* (Penguin Books, 1967). The author states that feudalism existed in Imperial China, and shows how it operated. See especially pp. 30—31.
45. Frank, A. G., *Capitalism and Underdevelopment in Latin America . . .*, op.cit., p. 224.
   Stavenhagen, Rodolfo, *Social Classes in Agrarian Societies,* (Anchor Books, Garden City, New York, 1975). Stavenhagen makes the following comments on page 12:
   . . . Dualism has indeed been the result of the establishment of capitalism, but not because the externally oriented modern sector has left the rest of the country behind. The traditional sector is itself a result of capitalist development. In fact, the externally oriented modern sector has subordinated the backward sector to serve its own interests. British colonial policies destroyed native manufactures and a self-sufficient agricultural village economy in India. Colonial practices in Africa disorganized precolonial tribal societies and created vast, impoverished reserves of labor for capitalist mines and plantations.
46. Mafeje, Archie., op.cit., pp. 31—32.
   Carter, Ian, "The Highlands of Scotland as an Underdeveloped Region", in *Sociology and Development*, edited by Emanuel de Kadt and Gavin Williams, (Tavistock Publications, 1974). On page 295, Carter points out that ". . . one of the problems of this school (Gunder Frank's et al) is that the difference between merchantilism and capitalism is never clearly specified—if, indeed, they accept the existence of such a difference."
47. Mafeje, Archie, op.cit., p. 46.
48. In his studies of West Africa, Samir Amin has suggested that some feudal social

formation had emerged in some of these states, but warns that these formations cannot be equated with the European feudal structures which preceded Western capitalism. See page 108 footnote 69 below.

49. Mafeje shows some of the differences that existed among the states of East and Central Africa:

    Zambia was dominated by the copper mining industry, and because there were only a few settlers along the line of rail, there was no significant land alienation.

    Kenya experienced some large-scale land alienation, especially in Kikuyu country where white settler determination to maintain their vested interests eventually led to the Mau-Mau Rebellion of 1952—56. Kenya was also dominated by the plantation economy.

    Rwanda-Burundi, Uganda, and *Tanganyika,* were dominated by the plantation economy. In Rwanda-Burundi (now forming separate states of Rwanda and Burundi), the Belgian colonial administration *forced* the Africans to produce cotton, and this together with the great land-hunger, compelled large numbers of Africans to migrate to neigbouring Uganda and Tanganyika. In the latter, now Tanzania, Africans were also *forced* by the German colonial administration to produce cash crops, an event believed to have led to the Maji-Maji Rebellion in 1905. (See pp. 42—43.)

    Campbell, Bonnie, "Neocolonialism, Economic Dependence and Political Change: A Case Study of Cotton and Textile Production in the Ivory Coast 1960 to 1970", *in Review of African Political Economy, No. 2,* (January—April 1975). Among other things, Campbell shows that French colonial policies which were similar to those just described above, have not changed with the declaration of independence. On page 37, Campbell writes:

    > During the years immediately following the Second World War, trade continued to reflect the classic pattern: the exchange of raw material (cotton) for finished manufactured products (textile goods). In order to increase the supply of colonial raw materials, *cotton production was forcibly imposed on many French overseas colonies by the colonial administration* . . . (My emphasis.)

    > During the post-independence period, the production and sale of cotton in the former colonial areas, remained in the hands of the same French companies. The creation of the newly formed state in no way altered the monopolistic organization of production and distribution. On the contrary the creation of an Ivorian marketing board and the new state's mediation between peasant producers and the French companies helped to smooth over the contradictions created by this organization of production (p. 38).

50. Barber, William, *The Economy of British Central Africa: A Study of Economic Development in a Dualistic Society,* (Stanford University Press, 1961) p. 4.

51. Quoted in Walter Elkan's "The Dualistic Economy of the Rhodesias and Nyasaland", a review article of Barber's book, in *Economic Development and Cultural Change, Vol. XI, Number 4* (July 1963) p. 445. On the same page, Elkan adds the following comments:

    > If there exists two kinds of books, those which pose and seek to answer questions, and those which explore what modifications are needed to make a model fit the facts, then Professor Barber's book belongs more to the second kind. It takes dualism as its model, and especially W. Arthur Lewis' fascinating articles on economic development with unlimited supplies of labour, and examines what reformulation may be necessary in order to make it convenient for work in Central Africa.

    But Arthur Lewis' "fascinating articles" have been criticised on very important grounds. For example, Mafeje, op.cit., page 37, has pointed out that

    > While aware of the unfavourable effect of foreign trade, Lewis is completely unaware of the negative dialectic of capitalist growth in ex-colonial or dependent

economies. Secondly, he minimizes the degree of integration of all sections of the population into capitalist production, *without its benefits.* He, therefore, sees underdevelopment as a passive state which could be activated by a strategic combination of conventional tools. (Emphasis in the original.)

52. Barber, W., op.cit., pp. 22—23.

III Community Development: A Critique

Although sociologists have, and continue to show interest in "peasant studies" and the general problems of rural development, the notion of community development has received less attention than it really deserves. This notion deserves greater attention than has been given because its protagonists have presented community development as a "model" specially designed and suited for the development of the rural areas in underdeveloped countries. Such studies of community development which have been undertaken have been dominated by social anthropologists, social workers and foreign "experts" usually associated with the administration of foreign aid programmes from the capitalist countries.[1]

A great deal of attention has, however, been paid to the other version of community development, namely "community work", and to "community studies", especially by British sociologists in reference to their own country. All these studies suffer from one major defect in common, and this is the tendency to see national and social problems in *local or personal* terms. In this, communities come to be seen in microscopic terms in which the physical or cultural characteristics become the focus of analysis rather than the problems of social and power relations, embracing both the internal and international systems.[2]

Community development is one of those ideologies which the independent states of tropical Africa have inherited from colonial rule, i.e. it is a branch of the *imported* theories of which a few have just been analysed in the foregoing pages. Therefore, community development must, like all other *export* models, be critically scrutinized to assess its alleged validity and relevance for the developmental needs and requirements of the independent states of tropical Africa.

This section of the paper opens with a brief description of the history of community development followed by a critical analysis of the *theory* and *methodology* of this concept.

History of Community Development

The notion of community development, as we know it today in tropical Africa and parts of Asia and Latin America, has a relatively short history. The notion was first conceived by the British colonial office, and it was from Britain that the community development model was later exported for use in British colonies. Peter Hodge, who shows that the concept of community development today is still confounded with confusion, also gives us an idea of its origin:

For the British this confusion may be partly explained by the fact that community development was an export model, first conceived in the 1920s by Colonial Officials and educationists to compensate for the shortcomings of the conventional school system in the former British dependent territories, as a vehicle for progressive evolution of the peoples to self-government in the context of social and economic change. Formal education in the schools had been thought by the missionaries and colonial officials to be the key to general progress until experience taught that to achieve the advancement of the whole community there was need, in addition to an improved system of schools, improvement in what today would be termed, other *nation-building proframmes for health, industry, agriculture and civic education.* Decades later, now that community development has been found to be *relevant to the social situation in the metropolis*—empire and dependent territories having passed into history—the concept has undergone a time- and sea-change.[3] (My emphasis.)

From this statement there are two more important points to note, namely that community development was originally designed for the particular "development" of colonial territories, and that therefore this method was not thought relevant for use in the metropolis. And secondly, we get some idea of the goals of community development, namely its role in the creation of future social institutions in the post-independence period.

It is of interest to note that although the notion of community development was first conceived in the 1920s, it was not until the 1940s that the British started exporting the model for application in their African dependencies.[4] The implantation of the model took place after a series of conferences on community development were held under the sponsorship of the Colonial Office. The most important of these conferences was held in 1948, and according to a United Nations Report, it was after this conference that the concept of community development became more clearly formulated and articulated. The blue-print which resulted from this conference was then sent to colonial administrators who were instructed to put this into effect. Part of the formulation of the concept reads as follows:

The dispatch was addressed to the Governors of the African Territories and was designed to dispel misunderstanding on the meaning of mass education. It supplied a definition and recommended that mass education or community development now be placed in the forefront of each colony's development policy along with the development of local government. It explained that mass education was neither an inferior substitute for education in the formal sense or a completely new system of administration.[5]

The fact that in this dispatch community development is seen as being related both to mass education and public administration has only added to the general confusion in the concept of community development. More will be said later about this when we discuss the relationship between community development and social work.

The response by colonial governors and administrators to the various conferences on community development in general, and the 1948 dispatch in particular, can be illustrated by several examples. Two examples from the British colonies of tropical Africa will suffice: According to Mulube, in Zambia (then

40

Northern Rhodesia) the 1940s saw the establishment of "Development Areas" by the British colonial administration.[6] These areas were selected in each of the provinces into which the country had been divided.

Mulube states that in 1943 the colonial government appointed a "Commissioner for Native Development" whose primary function was the supervision of "Development Area Schools" which had been set up in these areas. The main skills taught at these schools were house-building, capentry, shoe-repairing and various kinds of handicrafts. The purpose of the training itself was that the recruits would, after their training, return to their respective home districts and communities to impart their newly acquired skills to their people, thus enabling "development" to take place. Mulube concludes, predictably, that this attempt at community development was a complete failure because the individuals who were trained in those schools went to the towns to seek employment for their own advancement rather than return to their communities or villages.

The second example we cite is taken from Ghana (then the Gold Coast), and here Peter du Sautoy shows that there had been no effort by the British administration toward internal development before the end of the Second World War,

> ... but at the end of the war, with new horizons opening up, the then Gold Coast Government began to look towards development and expansion. Education was regarded as the key factor and already people were beginning to wonder whether some adult literacy might not be possible ... Some practical action was decided upon and the Gold Coast Government appointed a Social Development Officer. In 1948, Mr. A. G. Dickson (M.B.E.), was appointed and arrived in the country.[7]

The Ghana example is also important in another respect, namely that it set the pace for the rest of British colonial Africa. As Mason shows,

> The experience of Ghana is relevant here, for it was in Ghana where a national organization for community development and social welfare was first fully developed. In 1951, Ghana launched a five year programme for mass literacy and mass education comprising literacy campaigns, home economics, extension work for women, a programme of aided self-help, and provition for setting up a 'common-service' organization for extension campaigns.[8]

This first experiment is claimed to have been so successfull that the idea of community development soon spread beyond Ghana's borders to the French territories where it was immediately adopted and put into practice.[9]

It is hoped that this brief account of the history of community development will provide us with an adequate background for a more detailed analysis of the concept of community development and its implications for African development and change which now follows.

Definitions

A vast literature on community development has accumulated since the notion was first conceived. And, in keeping with this ever-increasing literature, a multitude of definitions of the concept have been formulated. Various definitions also exist for the term "community" as well. To refer to the contradictions in the existing definitions of community development as "confusion", as Hodge does, is certainly an accurate observation but quite clearly an under-statement. Hodge is also correct in suggesting that further attempts by authors to interpret existing definitions or formulate new ones merely add more confusion than clarity. He declares that

Confusion about the subject has also been compounded by the tendency for authors of standard text to recite the many definitions of community development and then to formulate another concoction of their own. More muddle has arisen from the recent use of 'community work' as an umbrella term—dustbin would be the more apt metaphor—to describe a wide spectrum of social and educational work with communities. 'Community work' is a compromise label because practitioners and pedants have been unable to evolve and agree on satisfactory interpretations, valid in British experience, of the better known process of community development and community organization. And calling down a plague upon both are the activists and conflict-mongers of 'community action'.[10]

The importance of this statement lies in the fact that it draws attention to the different approaches to the concept of community development by *conservative* and *radical* writers which is contained in the last sentence of the passage. The rest of this statement refers to the preoccupations with semantics among liberal writers themselves, a preoccupation in which what should be the central issues in the analysis are frequently avoided or mentioned only in passing.

Community development is a world-wide movement which has gained acceptance in most of the so-called "free world" (including the United Nations). Some of the claims of community development, the assumptions underlying its conception, as well as its internal contradictions, are revealed in its definitions. The following example can be taken as representative. According to this, du Sautoy defines community development as

...A movement designed to promote better living for the whole community with the active participation and, if possible, on the initiative of the community, but if this initiative is not forthcoming spontaneously, by the use of techniques for arousing and stimulating it in order to secure the active and enthusiastic response to the movement.[11]

du Sautoy cautions, however, that the pace towards the achievements of these goals should be *gradual* and the torch-bearers of the movement must adopt the slogan "improvement of the traditional". He asserts that "people who live in compound-style houses will not take readily to modern blocks of flats", after all, concludes du Sautoy, "community development deals with simple things and unsophisticated people ..." du Sautoy, who is aware of the contradictions in the various definitions and shows the factors which they have in common:

42

In all these definitions we can trace certain common factors. The most important is self-help. The second is that the initiative should come from the people themselves and not be imposed from above. The third is that there must be a process of stimulation by the community development organization to *break down apathy and to show the people that what they want can be provided, if they were prepared to listen to new ideas, and to help themselves.*[12] (My emphasis.)

The concepts of self-help, initiative and mass organization (mass mobilization) which are mentioned in this passage will receive detailed analysis in their own right later.

The second example of the definition of community development is that provided by the United Nations. In this case the author is referring to the way in which British Colonial Officials defined the concept. And according to this version the term

Community development has to do with getting backward people in the right frame of mind for doing things. It also has to do with 'social disequilibrium, sense of frustration, of inferiority and even of persecution'. . . . Politically, community development sets out to achieve a hopeful 'climate' in which government and people may cooperate and human capacity be developed. In Cyprus, Fiji, Aden, East and Central Africa, the West Indies and Malaya, community development is concerned with hastening the processes of unifying the various communities within a plural society. This includes attempts to find motives within the various societies and to initiate processes therefrom that may prove strong enough to remove group fears.[13]

In other parts of this UN Report from which this quotation is taken, reference is made to the effect that community development has to do with the creation of "social climate or a mental atmosphere 'favourable to the growth of *free institutions and mature personalities*'", and lays great emphasis on the factors of *cooperation and self-help*.[14] (My emphasis.)

The UN Report points out, by way of criticism, that "the concept of mass education, while it served a particular phase, was essentially a contradiction in terms. Community development with its emphasis on communal cooperation, initiative and self-help has tended so far to overlook the problem of the maladjusted individual." This is a misplaced criticism by the authors of this report because, on the contrary, and despite its collectivistic rhetoric, community development over-stresses individual problems at the direct expense of social problems. The real contradiction insofar as education is concerned, lies in the fact that while colonial education was supposed to be for the masses, this educational system was never meant and designed for mass consumption both in its *content* and quantity.

But having offered this "criticism" on the definition of community devolopment, how does the UN itself understand the concept? To the UN,

. . . Community development is a *technique* for improving the levels of living, particularly in underdeveloped areas, community development being interpreted as a *process creating conditions of economic and social progress* for the whole community with its active participation and the fullest possible reliance upon the community's initiative.[15]

43

It is hardly necessary to point out that this concoction too, in no way differs from the other definitions we have just seen. It erroneously reduces the socio-economic problems faced by underdeveloped countries into a "technical" question, while the goals of its efforts are described in abstract and vague terms as "creating conditions of economic and social progress".

Community

A great deal of confusion and controversy also surrounds the concept of community in community development literature. Peter Hodge has demonstrated the extent of this controversy by citing figures which show, among other things, that even within one and the same country, the size of community as a viable unit for community development programmes may vary considerably from one area to another.[16]

The major defect in the concept of community, as we have already pointed out, is the fact that communities are viewed as being composed of small groups of people, living in isolated villages and characterised by the so-called face-to-face relationships.

Even the UN Report just cited above is highly critical of the ways in which the term "community" is frequently defined in community development literature. While the authors of this report agree with the fact that due attention must be paid to small communities in every nation's development planning, the report argues against the narrowness of the definitions.[17] We cite at length some of the pertinent remarks made by the authors of this document:

A widening of the conception is needed also because both the range of interest and the range of competence often extended beyond the smaller community. Hence, while 'social progress through local action' is of great importance, the very proper emphasis on local participation in decisions, and on self-help activities, should not be pushed to the neglect of action by and through wider geographical communities or wider functional groups which are not local in the accepted sense of the word. On the contrary, it should be clearly recognized that there are definite limits to what smaller local communities can do, and that administrative viability alone demands a wider conception. A cumulative process of economic and social improvement, as distinct from once-for-all improvement of limited scope, is impossible simply on the basis of self-help, even though this is a necessary ingredient. It is useful to reiterate this rather obvious proposition because, as has come to our attention, neglect of it may lead to a *false dichotomy between the small local community and the territorial or national community or its government.*

... There is not so much dichotomy, as a composite process requiring that national and local programmes are not inconsistent but complementary, and that the technical and material resources of the wider community are made available.[18] (My emphasis.)

The real significance of this statement lies in its recognition of the fact that *community or social problems* cannot be understood outside the central question of the existence of *unequal access* to the foci of political power and the decision-making institutions of the nation by different groups of which society is composed. The colonial situation is an extreme example of political domination in which the whole of the colonized community is excluded from the nation's decision making processes. The effects of this exclusion have been succinctly described by Albert Memmi, when he stated that

The most serious blow suffered by the colonized is being removed *from history and from the community*. Colonization usurps any free role in either peace or war, every decision contributing to his destiny and that of the world, and all cultural and social responsibility.[19] (My emphasis.)

The new "social science" of community development promises, among its limitless objectives, as we shall see further, to *restore* the ex-colonial citizen to his rightful position in which, once again, so we are told, he will become a *maker of his own history.*

Theory of Community Development

One of the chief exponents of the community development movement, Pierre de Schlippe, opens his discussion on the history of community development by stating categorically that "A theory of community development does not exist". From here, de Schlippe proceeds to formulate such a theory. What is the theory of community development then, as formulated and elaborated by de Schlippe and his contemporaries?[20]

An examination of this formulation of de Schlippe, however, not only shows that de Schlippe and his contemporaries have utterly failed in producing the theory of community development, but it also reveals that the community development movement has ideological and political functions in the underdeveloped countries where the model is destined for application. All this will become abundantly clear as we proceed with our analysis.

First, it is necessary, however, to show how de Schlippe himself conceptualizes the notions of community development and community before we go into the analysis of his theory. de Schlippe accepts, without any questioning, the definition of community development as formulated above by the United Nations (p. 44), only adding that the ultimate aim of this process is to enable communities "to contribute fully to national progress".[21]

Although de Schlippe recognizes the need (as the UN does) for broadening both the concept and definition of the term "community", his own definition turns out to be no better or different from those which he is trying to discredit. He states:

The community is a social group which revolves round a certain number of economic activities and social services, generally a market, a church, a school, a dispensary, or a club.

In special cases it may be centered around an irrigation dam, a dipping tank for cattle, a common grazing area, a certain industry, or around common security precautions, as a wall, a police station, a fire brigade, and last but not least, around a council and an an administrative set. The minimum size of a community will be determined by these activities and services. The maximum size will be determined by the *number of people who can co-operate without spliting into subgroups* (social and professional stratification—in urban areas) or by the densitty of the population and by walking, riding, driving distance, the density finding its limit in the 'carrying capacity of the soil'. (Rural communities.)[22] (My emphasis.)

Apart from insisting and stressing that the ideal size of a community is one that is generally characterized by "face-to-face" relations, de Schlippe demands that the maximum size of a community must be determined by the needs for *co-operation* and *consensus*. By insisting on these factors as preconditions for an establishment of what should be a viable community, de Schlippe and his contemporaries are stressing the *social control role* of community development. Writing on this important aspect of community development, a former community development adviser to several African countries, including Zambia and the Cameroon, has stated:

It is felt that the contribution that community development can make to *good order, progress, and stability* of such countries is vital, and that to ignore the possibilities of this contribution could be a serious error. At the same time it would be unwise, perhaps, for Government openly to publicize the *functions of the Department of Community Development* from the angle described briefly above, since such publicity might draw towards the movement the hostility of possible dissident or opposition elements, whose interests might lie in an unstable and dissatisfied milieu rather than in a *progressive, stable and developing society.*[23] (My emphasis.)

When he looks at community development specifically from the ideological perspective, de Schlippe asserts that it is both a scientific and an ideological movement of world-wide dimensions. He does not only presents community development as a panacea for all the problems of underdevelopment but de Schlippe sees and will accept no other alternative theory of development and change. He rejects "dialectical materialism" or "Marxist socialism" out of hand as something utterly repulsive. de Schlippe proceeds to show that one of the *major tasks* of community development is the elimination of the Marxist method of social analysis which poses as an alternative to the functionalist method in the guise of community development. He declares in no uncertain terms:

Dialectical materialism, 100 years old and insufficiently based on knowledge of social science, has become another ethnocentric dogma which is not compatible with democracy. Its scientific character needs new emphasis (by those who still half profess it.) ... 'Agreements between minds can be reached spontaneously, not on the basis of common speculative ideas, but on common practical ideas'. Inductive theory, not deductive dogma, should be established. With the advantage of 12 years of accumulated experience, we shall try to do this now. We shall remain aware of limitations and try not to fall once more into the temptation of dialectical, dogmatic, deductive thinking.[24]

These attacks by de Schlippe are not merely directed at "dialectical material-ism" as such, but they are aimed at the whole body of Marxism, which, with one stroke of the pen, de Schlippe reduces to a mere dogma. Dialectical materialism is somehow seen as the embodiment of Marxism most probably because it stresses *contradiction* in social analysis, and as such it must be seen as posing immediate danger to the politics of *stability and consensus.*[25]

It is also of significance that de Schlippe, in his attacks on Marxism, singles out dialectical materialism but completely ignores *historical materialism.* By so doing he makes it easy for himself to label dialectical materialism as being specu-lative, deductive and dogmatic. Historical materialism, he would have found out if he had taken the trouble to do so, demands and insists that investigation on social, economic, political and cultural change and development must be based on the concrete, *historical settings and conditions.* In describing dialecti-cal materialism as being based on speculative ideas, de Schlippe conveniently forgets that Marx ". . . was not concerned either with the ontological problem of the relation of thought and being, or with problems of the theory of knowl-edge. Speculative philosophy of this kind was what Marx *rejected* in order to substitute science for metaphysics in a new field of knowledge."[26] (Emphasis in the original.)

de Schlippe's assertions raise further questions on the nature of dialectical materialism and Marxist dogmatism which require further comment and clari-fication. We shall return to these issues at a later stage in our analysis.

The ideological objectives of the community development movement are elaborated further by J. A. Ponsioen, one of de Schlippe's collaborators. He too is quite explicit on this point:

Community development is not only a method of development, it also shows many charac-teristics of a social movement, which spreads a kind of ideology throughout the world. The ideology of community development *rejects the authoritarian way of developing countries —the soviet approach*—and the individualistic way through competition for material wel-fare— as was the Western approach. The ideology of community development appeals to the citizens of a community to develop their own initiatives.[27] (My emphasis.)

And stressing the "absence" of contradiction, antagonism or conflict in com-munity development, de Schlippe claims that this is an "integrated" approach in which all aspects of community life will develop simultaneously in a balanced way.[28] This "balanced" development is assured, de Schlippe argues, because community development is an "intentional, guided, purposeful and target di-rected social change". And while de Schlippe recognizes the existence of in-equalities and even exploitation in different societies, he is at pains to gloss over these problems.

Over-simplistic and idealistic solutions are offered against the problems of class antagonisms, which he indirectly acknowledges. For example, according to de Schlippe, those groups in society which hitherto have been deprived of their democratic rights, will, in the era of community development, simply be granted these rights and privileges. Henceforth, problems of class antagonism will be solved, like with a magic wand, for example, "... by (the) separation of power, by opposing institutions (chief and council, factory-owner and trade union, landlord and tenants' association, cooperative societies etc.)"[29]

de Schlippe goes on to reassure us, in a manner not short of religious idealism, that when the "science" of community development has triumphed over dialectical materialism, a new social order will emerge in which society will be

Better according to various standards—bigger, wealthier, more productive, more co-operative, ... more ethical, more beautiful, and more free.[30]

And de Schlippe, of course, insists that all these prophetic predictions are based not on deductive, dogmatic and speculative ideas, but on solid, inductive theory of social science! He concludes with a stern warning, however, that the survival of this new social order will depend on the ability of the rulers in ensuring that the new freedoms are given in the appropriate dosages, as it were, and with the necessary safeguards. He betrays an unusual degree of fantasy as well as an overwhelming antagonism for what he terms "totalitarian socialism" and "communism", when, in the following passage, he equates these systems with *fascism* and *colonialism*:

The degree of freedom, initiative and participation, within purposeful, intentional or guided cultural development, is of greatest importance. Politically, after the period of unbridled private initiative as a thesis (capitalism), and a complete subjugation for the sake of guidance as antithesis (totalitarian socialism, fascism, communism, colonialism), the community development movement appears as a synthesis, a middle road, a movement of common sense and decency. A great task will consist of avoiding a lapse once more into extremes.[31]

This is the sum total of the theory of community development which de Schlippe has set out to formulate and crystallize: quite evidently, de Schlippe has only succeeded in demonstrating that community development has no scientific basis and that it is only of use to its protagonists as an ideological and political *weapon*.

The Methodology of Community Development

Does a methodology of community development, on which its claim to a scientific standing is party based, actually exist? J. A. Ponsioen, who sees community development as a method of developing the rural areas, believes that a methodology of community development exists. This method, according to him, has its origins from two main sources, namely the *social work method* and modern *public administration*.

This suggests that in order to understand the methodology of community development, we need to know something about the method of both social work and public administration. Ponsioen describes in sufficient detail how the social work method works. The essence of his analysis is contained in his summary conclusions in which he states that

Therefore, social work is a psychological approach to evoke, stimulate and activate the creativity and sociability of the assisted in order to enable them to solve their own problems by their own forces or by environmental forces invoked by themselves ... The process helps to *reinforce the client's personality*.[32] (My emphasis.)

Ponsioen then proceeds to elaborate on the psychological techniques used in the social work method. This enables him to establish, among other things, that there is a clear and natural link and compatibility between the social work method and the community development method. He describes this link unequivocally as follows:

What, in social work, is applied to individuals and groups, is applied by the community development method to communities. The principles, methods and techniques are essentially the same, although they are differentiated by the fact that a community is always composed of heterogeneous elements, and expresses itself through leaders. In community development, however, the approach should be combined with that of good public administration.[33]

Once having established the link between the methods of social work and community development, Ponsioen goes on to stress that the primary way by which community development "solves" socio-economic problems is through various psychological techniques because "it is evident that a programme of industrialization, a scheme of public works for land irrigation or a building up of a sanitation system, cannot be performed by the community development approach".[34]

But de Schlippe disagrees with Ponsioen. Writing in the same volume, de Schlippe claims that it is within the competence of community development to provide, for example, various kinds of new social services such as roads, markets, schools, dispensaries, irrigation schemes and even small-scale industries.[35] Furthermore, de Schlippe is in disagreement with Ponsioen in reference to the respective roles of community development and social work in the solution of social problems when he argues that

The role of social worker is not an integrated approach. The initiative rests with councils of local government. *The social worker is not an initiator, his role is remedial,* that of social assistance to existing authorities or to people grouping themselves around some problem. *One can hardly speak of community development at all.* Nevertheless it is this set of problems which have created the profession of social work, or the social assistant, and by imitation, this set of problems has been applied (and is still being applied) without further analysis to entirely different situations. Community development should eliminate this bias.[36] (My emphasis.)

Although de Schlippe gives the impression here, that he regards the social work method as obsolete, he fails to suggest a viable alternative, but only expresses the hope that community development will eliminate the bias inherent in social work, without, however, even indicating how this is to be done. While he clearly favours the community development approach to the social work method, de Schlippe fails to demonstrate exactly why community development should be preferred.

As if to show the insignificance of this "quarrel", de Schlippe, who sees problems of underdevelopment almost exclusively in cultural terms, comes to see community development in the end in the same terms as Ponsioen does. That is to say, that de Schlippe comes to see the principal role of the community development method as the *discovery* and *removal* of the supposed *psychological obstacles* that are alleged to inhibit the societies of underdeveloped nations from embracing and assimilating the "positive" cultural values of Western capitalist societies.[37]

Katayun H. Cama is another author who has collaborated with de Schlippe and Ponsioen in the formulation and articulation of the theory and methodology of community development.[38] Her own contribution is centered on the analysis of the relationship between social work and community development, paying particular attention to methods of training in both community development and social work and how the two types of personnel are supposed to function in practice.

Cama finds no difficulty in showing that the methods of training of social workers and community development workers are similar. The content of this training should be of interest to us since, through its examination, even only cursorily, we will then be able to judge if such a training is one likely to equip community development workers appropriately for the tasks they are supposed to perform in society. According to Cama, the content of training for community development workers (and social workers) consists in the following:

a) 'Imparting knowledge and information regarding human behaviour, the society and its culture pattern, the basic economic principles affecting the community and the administrative organization,
b) Teaching of skills which conveniently can be classified into i) *manipulative* and ii) skills in human relations,
c) Inculcating the *right attitudes*.'[39] (My emphasis.)

More similarities between the methods of social work and community development are listed by Cama when she discusses community development as a "process". What sticks out most prominently from Cama's analysis is the heavy emphasis on psychological techniques as the main characteristics of both the social work and community development approaches.[40]

Even when Cama occasionally shows some insight into the causes of social problems,[41] she fails to draw the correct conclusions, and thus erroneously looks to the social work and community development methods for possible solutions to the problems of underdevelopment.[42]

Having throughout stressed the necessity for professional training in both social workers and community development workers, and having succeeded in showing that there is no difference in both the methods and the training programmes of social work and community development, Cama subsequently tries to show that nonetheless, community development operates at a higher level than social work. This only leads to a lot of confusion in her analysis, highlighted by her final remark which is to the effect that, after all, the role of community development worker can be *fulfilled just as well by any general public administrator or government official* who happens to be easily available, especially in areas where professional community development workers are either in short supply or are not at all available.[43]

This discussion on the relationship between social work and community development has strongly emphasized the *psychological* aspects of this concept which *it has in common* with social work. This was necessary in order to refute the claims by the exponents of the community development movement that the latter has a scientific method of universal validity. However, I believe that the real or actual *mechanisms of the social control function* of community development are effected more effectively through its *administrative aspects* rather than through its *psychological manipulations of individual clients*. (See page 46 above.)

To illustrate the assertion just made, I will cite the example from Britain, where the 1960s saw great attempts to reform the country's social welfare model by shifting the emphasis, at least in theory, from previous preoccupations with individual problems, into more family and group oriented approaches.[44]

This shift took the form of structural changes in which the formerly fragmented social services were reunified under one powerful bureaucratic organization. While it was quite clear that such an upgraded administrative structure would, among other important things, considerably improve the career opportunities for social workers and "community workers", it was also claimed that this new social welfare organization would make provisions for participation by representatives of the recipients of social services (the consumers) in decision-making on matters which were of direct interest to them.[45]

This shift of emphasis, it must be stressed, did not question the efficacy of social casework as such. Its significance lay in the fact that it relegated the day to day contact with the clients largely to the junior staff, while the better or more highly qualified social workers were given the more *vital administrative* responsibilities. The director of the social services in the respective local authorities, was henceforth to be appointed on the basis of his *management* and *administrative* skills, in addition to his social work qualification, while his position was upgraded to more or less the same level as other top bureaucrats in the country.[46]

The real significance of these structural modifications of the social services in terms of the administrative control role of social work and community development, has been pointed out by A. H. Halsey, who has commented that

The apparatus of social administration, of which the academic wing is a relatively small one, *constitute a large vested interest in the status quo*. The young and impecunious

51

family caseworker will not easily see herself (or himself) as *the agent of an exploiting class. Nevertheless we cannot ignore the power of the interests of those who run the bureaucracies of welfare*—power which expresses itself ideologically if not materially in the shaping of policy and practice.[47] (My emphasis.)

Community Development and Public Administration

As it will be recalled, Ponsioen has suggested that public Administration was the second source from which the community development method owes its origin. An examination of the relationship between public administration and community development now follows. We make the assumption and stress in this analysis, that the *social control role* of community development will even become more prominent, especially under the umbrella of the national bureaucratic administrations known for their conservatism and commitment to the maintenance of the status quo rather than to innovation and change. We already know that in its inception by the British Colonial Office in the 1920s, community development was seen as an integral part of the existing colonial administration, even though it was relegated to a minor role, namely that of supplementing existing colonial institutions.[48] Contemporary supporters of the community development, including international organizations such as UNESCO, look upon it as an aspect of public administration. In many states of tropical Africa, departments of community development have been established in their own right.[49]

But once again, there is no agreement in this case among the protagonists of community development as to its objectives and aims as a method of public administration. The degree of confusion that we have come across in our discussion of the theory and method of community development is very much in evidence here too. There are also over-exaggerated claims about what can be achieved administratively through the method of community development.

Peter Kuenstler, whose views can be taken as representative on the subject, sees the relationship between community development and local government as being of several kinds: e.g., community development is a method merely of introducing a more formal system of local government; or it is a substitute for local government; or it is a parallel process—existing side-by-side with local government but maintaining its own autonomy, and finally, Kuenstler sees community development as a mere supplement to local government.[50]

Implicit in his description is the assumption by Kuenstler (and others) that the inherited colonial administrative structures are necessarily relevant to and meet the needs and requirements of the ex-colonial states of Africa and Asia. But even if these assumptions were to be accepted, the question would still arise as to why it then becomes necessary to create a "new" community development administration on top of the existing one? Furthermore, why should it be assumed without any questioning, as Kuenstler does, that the new community development administration would act as a corrective to the defects, inadequacy, inefficiency and other weaknesses which bedevil the existing, inherited administrations throughout tropical Africa?

In a closely argued paper entitled "Deadlock in Development Administration: The Community Development Approach", Bernard Schaffer exposes many of the inadequacies and shortcomings of this method. One of the main problems raised by Schaffer is the all important question of *client access* in public administration.

After a penetrating analysis of some of the main claims frequently made for community development as a method of public administration, Schaffer concludes that:

... the approach does not provide a solution for development administration partly because it is actually antiadministrative. That is so not so much because its frequent and apparently normative hostility to certain sorts of administrative agency and officials, on whom it happens, in fact, to rely. It is more because of its *ideological defences against evaluation and feedback*, the most urgent requirement of a development administration style. It also fails to provide a solution because it *seeks a mere blotting out of a problem*: on the one hand it seems to make evaluation unnecessary; on the other hand it sought, *not to solve the problem of communication, allocation and access*, but to be an alternative to administration.[51] (My emphasis.)

Evidence from most of the literature on community development show that one of the main preoccupations of community development agencies or programmes is the establishment of the so-called democratic institutions, and it is frequently the success in the erection of these structures which is equated with developmental achievement. In other words, when concrete evidence of the achievements of community development programmes are demanded, the exponents of the movement will often point to some village hall, club or other "recreational amenities", as the successes of community development which have been achieved through the people's own initiatives and on the basis of self-help. In some cases the list of community development projects undertaken will include streets, roads, schools, etc., all supposed to have been built on the basis of "voluntary" communal labour.[52]

But even more important is the frequent claim by community development "experts" that such projects as those mentioned above are relevant and constitute what they term the real needs of the local community concerned. There is abundant evidence, however, which shows that in many cases these community development projects are actually intended to serve the political and ideological interests of the sponsors rather than those of the villagers. A few examples will suffice to illuminate this fundamental problem: Peter du Sautoy, one of the zealots of community development, proudly reports that some villagers in Ghana (the Gold Coast), as a result of his own achievement in initiating the movement, built a road for his own personal use! He writes enthusiastically:

A three mile road to enable me to visit Nkwantia Village is under construction to join the Kintampo—Nkoranza motor road. Tools have been loaned by the District Development

Committee. Broahoho is building a village hall in cement blocks; 600 blocks are ready to date.[53]

Underlying this self-explanatory passage is the commonly held assumption that local people often do not know what their own problems are, and that even when they are aware of these problems, nothing gets done about them since these villagers lack the initiative. But this alleged lack of initiative in the local people has been shown to be false many a time. While du Sautoy was celebrating the "achievements" of his movement, Polly Hill shows that more significant initiatives were being undertaken in the same country:

The farmers, as businessmen, were unimpressed by the colonial administration and undertook their own development expenditure to provide better links between the cocoa forests and their homeland: Before 1914 the Akwapim farmers had hired contractors to build three bridges over the River Densu (being businessmen they recouped their expenses by charging tolls) and a little later they invested at least £50,000 in the building of motorable roads to Akwapim.[54]

An extensive study of community development programmes carried out in India a few years ago, shows even better, who the real beneficiaries of community development projects are.[55] Part of this study consisted of questionnaires about the usefulness or relevance of community development to the local people. Included also was the question of access to community development officials by the local people, and the responses to these and other questions are most instructive. Here is a sample of some of the questions that were posed, as well as the responses to them:

1) Do you think the community development programme is worthwhile or do you think the government should stop this programme? (Table 2.5, p. 21.)

The response to this question was that 67% of those interviewed said the programme was worthwhile; only 8% said it should be stopped, while 22% expressed no opinion. (2% were not ascertained.)

2) What in your opinion are the most important accomplishments of community development here (rural sample)? (Table 7.1, p. 119.)

The following responses were recorded to this question:

Nothing has been accomplished   22%
Don't know about accomplishments   42%
Mentions specific accomplishments   37%

Taking it for granted that the most ignorant villager would still be able to see or recognize any concrete changes if these had occurred in the village, then the correct interpretation of and conclusions to be drawn from, these responses is that the majority of respondents have in fact stated that "nothing has been accomplished". And, included in that majority must be the 42% of "don't knows" since there are many obvious reasons why many villagers often prefer to remain "neutral" for fear that it might not be safe for them to give a negative response to questions posed by government officials, including research workers.

When the 37% (Table 7.1, above) who had mentioned specific achievements of community development were then asked to point out some of these achievements, the following picture appears:

Streets, roads mentioned   33%
Water and irrigation mentioned   22%
Agricultural assistance mentioned   21%
Schools mentioned   15%
Health improvements mentioned   8%

Further questions that must be asked in reference to these responses are, for example, the basis of labour—whether it was "voluntary" or paid, and this is important especially in view of the fact that the construction of streets and roads tops the list. Another key question to ask is whether or not the different social strata have equal access to the use of irrigation water, agricultural assistance and health services. Answers to some of these questions are provided below (p. 60).

One more important question remains to be examined from this study, and this is the question of contact or communication between community development officials and the people they are supposed to assist. The study shows that in a sample of 335 cases, *66% had never had any contact* with community development officials, and out of 208 farmers, *59% had never had any contact* with community development officials. These figures, which pertains within the lower stratum of the farming community, contrast sharply with the situation within the upper stratum of the farming community.

In other words, access to community development officials was determined by the relative social standing of the two major groups within the farming community. This is demonstrated by the fact that between 50% and 70% of the upper income and well-to-do farming groups in India maintained constant contact with community development officials while as much as 70% of the illiterate peasants and low income groups had no such contact.[56]

In the face of this evidence, the authors of this study who had set out to prove that community development as a modern "democratic" institution, was relevant for the socio-economic development and administrative requirements of India, were compelled, at least in reference to the problem of communication, to conclude that

... But for a developiny society which has stacked much of its plans or programmes requiring public information, instrumental knowledge, and understanding of its goals, our findings on the level of public knowledge are disillusioning. Our data suggest a serious communication gap between the planners and a majority of the Indian rural, and probably the urban, public.[57]

But nevertheless, the authors of this study do not think that there is an alternative to the community development method. They view these failures as unavoidable or even as necessary "birth pangs" in the creation of a new institution whose "aspirations and plans" will "gradually percolate downward through the social status hierarchy.[58]

Initiative, Felt needs and Self-help

As we have already seen, there is hardly any definition or discussion of community development which does not include at least one of these three concepts. The usage of these concepts in community development literature represent nothing less, though in a different guise, than the well-known *politics of individual freedom and competitive economic individualism* under the capitalist system.

We wish to point out, therefore, that our attempt to falsify the conservative assertions that so-called traditional people generally lack initiative and so forth, does not in any way suggest that we *subscribe to the usage* of these concepts by conservative writers or to the capitalist methods of development as such (see pp. 53—54 above).

INITIATIVE

By assuming *lack of initiative as an original state*, conservative social theory demonstrates ons of its major defects, namely its frequent failure to make a clear distinction between *cause* and *effect* in the analysis of social problems. This happens, for example, when certain sociological phenomena which can be objectively observed, for instance, when in a given poverty-stricken community it is observed that people generally appear to be lacking in initiative, or that they appear apathetic and lethargic, these observations are taken to be the explanation of the state of poverty within that community.

Once again it becomes necessary to dispel any possible misunderstanding of our position: our attempts to disprove conservative allagations and claims, does not constitute any intention on our part to deny the existence of apathy, lethargy, the lack of initiative or desire to participate in communal affairs, on the contrary, we believe that these phenomena exist in different communities, varying in degree and intensity according to the historical experience of a given community.

Failure to make a clear distinction between cause and effect in social analysis often leads to a situation in which social problems, for example poverty, come to be seen in terms of what has been called the "vicious circle of poverty".[59] Crudely stated, this would mean, in the present context, that lack of initiative, taken as an original state, leads to successive situations in which social problems are not tackled or solved; no improvements in the living conditions occur and with the latter leading to extreme poverty and misery. And finally, the circle closes since it would be unrealistic, so conservatives would argue, to expect poverty-stricken people to show anything other than lack of initiative, apathy, lethargy and so forth. This alleged vicious circle of poverty can be illustrated by this simple diagram:

Figure 2

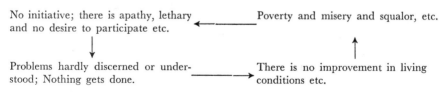

Conceptualizing social problems in this manner, as exponents of community development often do, there is no wonder therefore, that they are unable to find ways of *breaching* this man-made circle of poverty. When the usual psychological "solutions" suggested by community development experts fail to liberate people from apathy, lethary and so on, it is the victims themselves who are blamed.[60]

The negative role of existing social institutions and the community leadership in blocking the release of initiatives from the community has either been ignored or greatly underrated. However, it has been shown time and again, how the process of community development has acted to inhibit rather than promote favourable conditions in which the desired socio-economic development and changes could occur. This point can be illustrated by an example from the UN Report we cited earlier. This is the instance in which officials engaged in a community development experiment in Udi (Eastern Nigeria) had found it very difficult to recruit *unpaid labour* for some of their projects.

This problem, however, was quickly solved as soon as some reforms were introduced into the system of "native administration", i.e., when the British started to prepare Nigeria for eventual political independence. The Report concludes, significantly that

The 'indigenous organization with its age grades that are responsible for communal labour ... is still for the most part intact. The experiment has not created community spirit. That spirit was there all the time.' The removal of inhibitions gave it free play.[61]

FELT NEEDS

A distinction is often made by community development theorists and practitioners between what they term "felt needs" and "real needs". The implication of this dinction becomes clearer when community development exponents proceed to claim and try to show that the villager is often not in a position to know his "real needs" which he should legitimately try to satisfy, from his "felt needs", which are said to be unrealistic or even utopian.[62] This being the case, the argument continues, it becomes the responsibility of the social worker or community development worker to help the villagers become aware of their so-called real problems or needs.

This subtle distinction of human needs into two apparently distinct categories may seem so superficial as to require no special consideration. However, this distinction implies, in fact, an important contradiction between the interests of the community on the one hand, and those of the ruling elements in society and their "external agents", on the other.

In his criticism of the concept of "cultural lag", Charles Erasmus simultaneously attacks the notion of felt needs as exposed in numerous literature on community development. He points out that:

From some points of view, a cultural lag may exist among backward people who have difficulty accepting new technologies. In this sense 'lag' may be just another way of expressing 'underdevelopment'. But when a group is unable to accept new techniques for so-called social reasons, *there is usually a vast difference between the felt needs of the innovators and those of the people to be changed. That is, the lag is really between the felt needs of the host group and those of the donors of technology.*[63] (My emphasis.)

In an analysis of India's rural development policy in the 1960's,[64] some social scientists have recently asserted that ". . . The Community Development Movement of the Indian Government is an attempt to bridge the gap between the ruling élite and the mass of the Indian people . . ." while another social scientist has described the same effort as a process of "betting on the strong". However, it is the latter analysis which shows more directly and more accurately what the real effects of this effort are, based as they are, on obvious *class* considerations. By the policy of "betting on the strong", W. F. Wertheim means that ". . . well-to-do farmers, some of them with sufficient education, and having come into contact with so-called 'modernizing élites' in the cities, were selected by the Government and given preferential treatment—they were freely supplied with fertilizers, improved seeds, technical advice and other forms of aid. It was assumed that the further progress these farmers would make would serve as a focus for imitation by the poorer farmers and the masses at large."[65] The result of this policy, as anyone would have expected, was the widening rather than the narrowing or bridging of the gap between the rich and the poor.

Apart from community development, there are other so-called new and modern democratic institutions which are supposed to work for the benefit of the community "as a whole", but in reality operate on the same principles of "betting on the strong". Of these, the cooperative movement has received a great deal of attention from social scientists. For example, Tamás Szentes has recently commented on the structure of cooperatives which, in Africa according to him, are mainly divided into marketing and/or credit institutions.[66]

Szentes shows that the aims of cooperatives in the African states differ from similar institutions found in many of the West European countries. In the latter countries the aims and objectives of cooperatives were to help smallholdings to compete more effectively against large estates, while in the independent African states the main aim of cooperatives is to support and encourage the production of commodity or cash crops on the basis of "private" or "individual initiative". This means that the cooperatives in fact operate for the further advancement of the so-called progressive or well-to-do farmers against the small and poor peasant producers.

Szentes also shows that in the African states both government policy and the policies and practices of the foreign-owned banking institutions give their support to the strong against the weak in the farming community. As a result of these policies, Szentes adds, the cooperative movement has already helped to create a stratum of rich farmers in Tanzania and other states; and since the control of these cooperatives is in the hands of the rich farmers, other benefits also accrue to its members, e.g., educational priviledges for the children of cooperative members.[67]

Wertheim criticises the assumption that cooperatives will provide a panacea against all the problems of underdevelopment in the ex-colonial territories as an example of yet another fallacy. From his comments, which we quote at length, we gain a clear picture of how cooperatives function, and why they cannot be expected to bridge the gap between the rich and poor strata of the underdeveloped nations:

... The cooperatives are mostly based on the 'betting on the strong' principle. Even if poor peasants are admitted as members, actual leadership of the cooperative is generally in the hands of wealthier landowners. The activities of the cooperatives will mostly benefit those who are already fairly prosperous. Moreover, the introduction of cooperatives in a society where private farming, private trade, and private money-lending are not abolished may produce a strange situation. A rich farmer, who is at the same time chairman of a cooperative, may channel the more profitable transactions to his private farm, leaving the less profitable ones to the cooperative. A private money-lender who is chairman of a cooperative may, in his latter capacity, extend loans to his solvent debtors in order to let them pay. Again, cooperatives function within a distinct social structure. Their existence in itself is not enough to help change the structure and to surmount its inequalities. On the contrary, the new institutions will be used by the existing power élite to further its aims, regardless of the egalitarian ideology professed by its propagandists.[68]

It is this outrageous and similar discriminatory policies and practices which explain, at least in part, the uncooperative attitudes sometimes shown by peasant producers towards government authorities. These attitudes have sometimes taken the form of rejecting government advice by the peasants, even when the acceptance of such advice would clearly have meant *extra cash* in the pocket of the small peasant producer. And yet, as D. W. Norman shows, social scientists have, surprisingly, frequently failed to comprehend the proper basis of such peasants' attitudes and behaviour.[69]

Accordingly, Norman warns against this simplistic approach which would interpret, for example, a refusal by peasants to cooperate with government authorities or experts in the production of cash crops as being *irrational* on the grounds that such behaviour is not consistent with the goal of profit maximization.

Basing his arguments on the findings of village surveys carried out in parts of the Northern states of Nigeria, Norman states that it was once recommended to the so-called subsistence farmers that they should plant their cotton crop early in May and June if they were to reap rich harvests. The peasant producers, however, all ignored this advice and continued to plant their cotton as usual in July. Norman shows that the real reason for this "irrational" behaviour was that May—June is the pick season during which *family labour, on which peasant farming is dependent,* was fully occupied in the production of food crops.

In an attempt to break this "resistance to change", so it would appear, the authorities in Northern Nigeria decided to increase the price guarantee of cotton by 25% during the 1968/69 season, but the peasants did not change their practice; i.e., they did not change in the way the authorities had expected and hoped. What the peasants did in response to these substantial economic incentives was simply to increase the acreage under cultivation but leaving the planting to take place in July as before. From this observation, Norman concludes that:

Such a strategy would have interfered with their goal of security and perhaps would force them to sacrifice some of their food crops. Thus farmers do respond to economic incentives as other research workers in Africa have found. However, at this point a note of caution may not be amiss. Farmers do and will respond to new technology and incentives but it is a response conditioned on the provision that it will not conflict with the over-riding goal of security with its non-economic facts.[70]

In some parts of India, to cite another example, it was observed that the small peasant producers did not seem to be interested in using water to irrigate their plots when the Indian Government had made this available to the "whole" farming community. This was then blamed on the alleged ignorance, apathy and even laziness of the peasants who were now said to be demonstrating their resistance to change. The fact of the matter was, however, that the small peasant farmer was required to dig a ditch leading from the main canal in order to get the water to his own plot. And it was where such a ditch had to be cut through the land of a big landowner where the peasant did not dig the ditch, and this was because the big landowner exacted a tax for the use of the ditches, a tax which most poor peasant producers could not afford.[71]

SELF-HELP

As we have already indicated, we do not subscribe to the way concepts such as "self-help" are used or applied in community development literature (page 40 above). In the rural areas of tropical Africa, competitive economic individualism was promoted and supported by colonial regimes through their encouragement of commodity or cash crop production, i.e., in those situations in which peasants were not openly forced to produce cash crops. In our opinion, the positive concept of self-help (self-reliance), in the context of the socio-economic problems of underdeveloped countries, has relevance only when it suggests the need for the entire internal social system to be self-reliant, i.e., the need for self-liberation from foreign domination. There can be no truly self-reliant communities whose national economy is controlled by external interests.[72]

Some of the internal contradictions in the concept of self-help as used in community development literature have been strongly criticised by Charles Erasmus, who refers to the "anachronistic" procedures in self-help in the following way:

In practice, a common sequitur of self-help emphasis of community development is the recapitulation of the 'house-hold economy' by teaching poor families such self-sufficient skills as canning their own food, sewing their own clothes, making their own furniture. ... Throughout rural Venezuela I found farm wives being taught by home demonstrators to weave handbags they are unable to sell and not interested in using.[73]

One of the main claims of community development is that through self-help, through communal, voluntary cooperation, communities not only can improve their living conditions, but they can make a worthwile contribution to the national economy. Once more, Erasmus remains unconvinced, and goes on to raise a pertinent question:

Why make families more self-sufficient in countries struggling to expand internal markets? When people begin buying television sets and other manufactured goods, the occupational structure is on the road toward greater diversification. If growing urban populations are to be employed, *national industries catering* to expand consumer demands—particularly within the large rural sectors—should be encouraged. *Any government promoting the house-hold economy works against itself* ... Many of the self-help objectives of community development fit best in a Paleolithic context.[74] (My emphasis.)

We have seen in the foregoing pages how much the psychological aspects of the community development movement have been stressed by the movement's protagonists. Erasmus shows how the notion of changing "the inside where it matters", has increasingly gained support, at least from US supporters of the movement. He writes:

Community development without tangible results is now so acceptable it can be publicly advertised at public expense. And should any academic consultant to the U.S. foreign aid programme suggests that the emperor has no clothes, his report can be classified to prevent its publication. National level strategy is much the same. As the community development literature indicates, desirable local 'leadership' is not spontaneous. Moreover, the host government personnel participating in community development projects are usually part of that middle sector phenomenon called the 'new élite'. Government employment offers most of these people economic and political opportunities greater than they can find via those routes we consider entrepreneurial.[75]

Conclusion

From the foregoing critique of community development, the conclusion is inescapable that this model, which has neither theory nor methodology of its own, has no relevance for the developmental needs and requirements of the underdeveloped states of tropical Africa. However, some critics of this model still seem to believe that this model might still have some usefulness provided that it first underwent radical structural changes. Among these, Gunder Frank,[76] has attempted to spell out what he believes are the necessary preconditions for the community development approach to become a relevant model that could be used as an effective instrument for delevopment and change in underdeveloped countries. Frank's preconditions, which we wish to adopt as our concluding remarks, can be summarised as follows:

1. The community development approach must seek a deeper understanding of social relations within communities and change these relations rather than concentrate, as it does, on the community's physical and cultural attributes. These are the social relations of production, distribution and exchange.

2. Community development programmes must, if they are to be successful, adequately mobilize and assist peasants and other underprivileged classes to effectively confront landlords, merchants and other privileged classes which oppress them. This is the only way to ensure popular participation by the masses in the economic and political processes of the nation. Peasants and other underprivileged groups have little or no bargaining power in contrast with the rivals in society.

3. Community development programmes must, if they are going to succeed, relinguish the practice through which they come to depend on "voluntary, cooperative, communal labour". Instead, they must rely on paid labour because the so-called voluntary labour is often a way of securing cheap labour by the authorities. As such this labour does not contribute to the release of the necessary initiatives and popular participation. Paid labour, according to Frank, necessitates, among other things, the establishment of trade unions. He states that ". . . This organization of 'participación popular' essentially involves the organization of labour unions and the provision of institutional framework through which the peasant can effectively act to coordinate his own with any public attempts to promote and protect the interests of increased peasant productivity and distributive justice."

4. *Rural Markets*. (i) Rural marketing organizations must not only be formed but they must have substantial representation from regional and local peasant organizations in addition to public officials appointed from the nation's capital on their own and regional policy-making boards. (ii) Foreign firms and corporations and their domestic subsidiaries must be prohibited from operating in rural and provincial markets to purchase staples and industrial or export crops for foreign or domestic sales. In Frank's view,

... the internationally derived financial strength of these foreign corporations generally involves them in national rural credit operations through which to their own, but not necessarily to the nation's, interest they can and do organize the selection, production, financing and marketing of major crop or crops of a whole region, country, or series of countries, and the promotion of industrial or export crops or livestock, to the prejudice of food crops needed for the provision of better diets for the rural and national population.[77]

5. Local communities must be assured of direct access to the foci of political power, including the national center. This accessibility would make it possible, for example, to take effective steps to redress the imbalance of bargaining power at local and regional levels. In connection with this important requirement, Frank suggests, furthermore, that the evaluation of the performance of community development programmes, presently in the hands of local élites, must be taken away from this group. This means that alternative channels of evaluation of these programmes through "participación popular" would have to be found.

These, then, are some of the main structural changes which, in Frank's view, the current concept of community development must undergo if the movement is to become relevant for the developmental needs and requirements of the underdeveloped countries of Africa, Asia and Latin America.

It would be an illusion to imagine that such radical transformation of the structure of community development could be envisaged or undertaken by the establishment, since such transformation poses a threatening challenge to the existing social relations which benefits the ruling classes. The oppressed who must initiate these changes must expect a great resistance and opposition from the establishment, and it is most important, therefore, that the peasants see their effort as part and parcel of the total struggle whose major goal is not only the transformation of a small part, but the eventual transformation of the entire socioeconomic system. Understood this way, "participación popular" becomes a dynamic process as part of the social and political mobilization which we discuss towards the end of this paper (page 98).

Notes

1. Foster, George, M., *Traditional Cultures: And the Impact of Technological Change* (University of California, Berkeley, 1962). This work is cited as a typical example of numerous studies of community development by social scientists involved in different ways with foreign aid for community development programmes. Among other things, Foster was consultant on Community development programmes of various underdeveloped countries, and has been special lecturer to the U.S. Peace Corps Volunteers.
2. Heraud, B. J., *Sociology and Social Work: Perspectives and Problems* (Pergamon Press, Oxford, 1970) pp. 6 and 93.
Frankenberg, Ronald, *Communities in Britain: Social Life in Town and Country*, (Penguin Books, 1966). Although Frankenberg adopts the so-called face-to-face approach in this study, this does not prevent him from recognizing what are the impor-

tant issues in the study of communities. This is because, or at least in large measure, due to the fact that, Frankenberg's views of community and social relations are, in my opinion, correct and therefore differ in important ways from those of most of the other writers in this field. He states, for example, on page 255:

> My view of class relations is essentially based on differing relationships to the means of production, that is to property, and in this I am following Marx. I am particularly interested in Marx's views on class for it was he who saw that the struggle between the classes created social change, and he was particularly concerned with the increasing divergence of rural and urban societies. His ideas and analysis are therefore helpful and relevant to my argument.

3. Hodge, Peter, "The Future of Community Development", in *The Future of the Social Services*, edited by A. Robson and B. Crick (Penguin Books, Harmondsworth, England, 1970) pp. 66—67.
    Buchanan, Keith, *Reflections on Education in the Third World* (The Bertrand Russell Peace Foundation, Spokesman Books, 1975) Buchanan writes on page 50:

    > It is one of the ironies of the colonial system that the *techniques of manipulation and coercion* used against colonial populations are, sooner or later, used by the government against the people of the metropolitan country. Thus, the techniques developed in the struggle against the Vietnamese are now used by the Americans against dissident groups in their own country ... etc. (My emphasis.)

4. Mason, Horace, "Community Development: Some Comments on the African Contribution", paper published by (Rural Development College, Holte, Denmark, 1965). Mason shows that it was no accident that the British felt the urgency of applying the community development model at that particular time. This was when the forces of nationalism were gaining momentum throughout tropical Africa, (p. 10).

5. *United Nations Series on Community Organization and Community Development, No. 21: A Study prepared For the UN,* by S. Milburn (New York, 1954—55) p. 24.

6. Mulube, Ernest, "The Role of Community Development in National Development". An unpublished diploma thesis in Social Policy (Institute of Social Studies, The Hague, 1969) pp. 6—13.
    Heisler, H., "Community Development or Development Administration in Zambia", in *Community Development Journal, No. 5, January 1967*, pp. 20—25.
    Mason, Horace, op.cit., pp. 1 and 3.

7. du Sautoy, Peter, *Community Development in Ghana* (Oxford University Press, 1958) p. 22.

8. Mason, Horace, op.cit., p. 8.

9. du Sautoy, P., op.cit., pp. 25—29. On these pages du Sautoy writes about the joint training programmes for community development workers between Ghana and the neighbouring French colony of Togoland.

10. Hodge, P., op.cit., p. 67.
    Albrow, Martin, "Dialectical and Categorical Paradigms of a Science of Society", in *The Sociological Review, Vol. 22, No. 2*, New series (University of Keel, May 1974), pp. 183—201.

Our aim in citing these different definitions is not an attempt to find or select the "correct one" among them, but we are doing this in order to bring out or expose the underlying assumptions of community development, as well as some of its main internal contradictions. And because I see my paper as an attempt to find an *alternative* approach to social analysis, I am aware of the dangers attendant to one's willingness to be lured into a position where one feels compelled, in the name of "clarity", to formulate *formal definitions* and models. In this connection, Martin Albrow (op.cit., page 183) has written:

> A dialectical approach in sociology is not often enough seen for what it is: *an alternative to the dominant orthodoxy in sociological method*. Indeed the very

use of the term 'dialectic' *tends to invite the side-tracking of the main issues by arousing pre-mature demands for precise definition or philological projects.* (My emphasis.)

11. du Sautoy, P., op.cit., p. 2.
    Clifford, W., "Community Development as a Movement and Philosophy", in *Social Research and Community Development*, edited by Raymond Apthorpe (Rhodes-Livingstone Institute, Lusaka, 1961).
12. du Sautoy, P., op.cit., p. 3.
13. UN Series on Community Organization and Community Development ... op.cit., p. 43.
14. Ibid., op.cit., p. 43.
15. *UN Series on Community Development, No. 26: Report on the Mission to Survey Community Development in Africa—January—April 1956* (New York, 15 August 1958) p. 21.
16. Hodge, P., op.cit., p. 68.
17. *UN Series on Community Development, No. 26, ...* op.cit., p. 25.
18. Ibid., op.cit., p. 25.
19. Memmi, Albert, *The Colonizer and the Colonized.* (Souvenir Press, London, 1974) p. 91. In reference to the problem of apathy, which conservative writers generally regard as *cause* rather than *effect or consequence*, Memmi blames this on the very fact that the colonized has been removed from history. As a result, "He (the colonized) has forgotten how to participate actively in history and no longer even asks to do so. No matter how briefly colonization has lasted, all memory of freedom seems distant ..." p. 92.
20. de Schlippe, Pierre, "The Theory of Community Development", in *Social Welfare and Policy: Contribution to Theory*, edited by J. A. Ponsioen (Mouton and Company, The Hague, 1962) p. 85.
21. Ibid., op.cit., p. 88.
22. Ibid., op.cit., p. 137.
23. Phillips, A. M., "The Contribution of Community Development to Political Stability", in *Community Development Journal, Vol. 4, No. 4,* (October 1969) p. 189.
    Schaffer, B. B., "The Bureaucratic Style of Administration", in *Politics and Change in Developing Countries: Studies in Theory and Practice of Development*, edited by Colin Leys (Cambridge, 1969) p. 196.
    Heraud, P. J., op.cit., p. 93.
24. de Schlippe, P., op.cit., p. 87.
25. Community development literature is replete with examples of development projects, so-called, designed to counter conflict and create and maintain "stability".
26. Bottomore, T. B., and Rubel, M., *Karl Marx: Selected Writings* in *Sociology and Social Philosophy*, edited. (Penguin Books, Harmondsworth, England, 1956) p. 36.
27. Ponsioen, J. A., "Community Development as a Process", in *Social Welfare Policy: Contribution to Theory*, op.cit., p. 52.
28. de Schlippe, P., op.cit., pp. 90 and 93.
29. Ibid., op.cit., p. 113.
30. Ibid., op.cit., p. 104.
31. Ibid., op.cit., pp. 141—142.
32. Ponsioen, J. A., op.cit., p. 51.
33. Ibid., op.cit., p. 51. Elaborating on the psychological methods of social work, Ponsioen states that these are:
    1) the establishment of a relationship of confidence with those to be assisted, that should be one of assistance and no more than that;
    2) the use of the relationship to induce the client to find out and formulate his own shortcomings (felt needs), and as far as possible, the cause of his needs

(real needs to him): the worker should not go further in trying to discover the real needs than can be discovered by the client;

3) the inducement of the client to find out and formulate what can be done to improve his situation; and

4) the inducement of the client to use his own initiative to mobilize his personal and environmental forces. The process helps to reinforce the client's personality, (p. 51).

34. Ibid., op.cit., p. 56.

35. de Schlippe, P., op.cit., p. 123.

36. Ibid., op.cit., pp. 120—121.

37. Ibid., op.cit., pp. 90—123. In conclusion, de Schlippe states on page142, that "in particular, Community Development is the movement which will bring the new universal values to every corner of the planet, adjusting them to local traditional values, and not to Western European ones (sic!)

Buchanan, K., op.cit. Against de Schlippe's day-dreaming, Buchanan has written: One set of values only is acceptable—the values of Western industrial society— and these values have universal validity, whether it be a question of models of economic development or of automobiles, soft drinks, housing styles or standards of feminine beauty. And nowhere is the thrust of this cultural imperialism or its results more evident than in the field of education. etc. (p. 36).

38. Cama, K. H., "The Role of training of Professional Social Workers for Community Development", and "Casework in Community Development Setting", in *Social Welfare Policy: Contributions to Methodology*, edited by J. A. Ponsioen (Mouton and Company, The Hague, 1963) pp. 9—32.

39. Ibid., op.cit., p. 11. Cama is quoting from a UN document entitled "Training for Social Workers: Third International Survey", (UN, 1958).

40. Ibid., op.cit., p. 13.

41. Ibid., op.cit., p. 29.

42. Ibid., op.cit., p. 17. On the same page, Cama writes:

Also, while social work is *palliative, ameliorative, preventive, curative, remedial, rehabilitative*, community development is concerned with improvement of of the quality of living of the community as a whole. The concept 'community' bears a sense of totality and wholeness as applied to people and to the facilities to be made available to them. As the skills required in community development are technical, educational, social and administrative, *the task of the social workers in learning to make the most effective contribution to community development, is to try to deepen their knowledge of the behavioural and social sciences, to refine their skills in working with groups and to sharpen their tools in dealing with communities.* (My emphasis.)

43. Ibid., op.cit., pp. 14 and 15 and 29.

44. *Report of The Committee on Local Authority and Allied Personal Social Services* (London, Her Majesty's Stationery Office, 1968). It is not without significance that the Chairman of the committee which drew up this report was Sir Frederic Seebohm, then Chairman of Barclays Bank, and most of the other members were highly placed social workers.

45. Sinfield, Adrian, "Which Way Social Work", in *The Fifth Social Service: Nine Fabian Essays*. (Fabian Society, London, 1970) pp. 23 ff.

Hodge, P., op.cit., p. 66.

46. Sinfield, A., op.cit., pp. 28, 43, and 50—51.

47. Halsey, A. H., "Social Science, Social Policy and Social Work", Paper read at the Nottingham Conference of the S.A.A., July 1969) p. 2.

48. *UN Series, . . . No. 21*, op.cit., p. 45.

49. Stavenhagen, R., "Changing Functions of the Community in Underdeveloped Coun-

tries", in *Underdevelopment and Development: The Third World Today*, edited by Henry Bernstein (Penguin Books, Harmondsworth, England, 1973) p. 93. Stavenhagen shows that big funds have been spent by such international organizations like UNESCO to help the community development movement expand its administrative activities.

50. Kuenstler, Peter, "Administration in Community Development", in *Social Welfare Policy: Contributions to Methodology*, edited by J. A. Ponsioen, op.cit., p. 135.
51. Schaffer, B. B., "Deadlock in Development Administration: The Community Development Approach", in Colin Leys (see footnote 23 above). In reference to the history and relevance of community development, Schaffer has commented as follows:

> ... Its origins were partly in colonial preparatory policy for local government and mass literacy education and in the American experience of agricultural extension and home economics taken together. Since decolonization, there has been a wide variety of experiments: clubs, village resettlement, low-level political institutionalization. *The approach looks highly relevant. The record shows that it has in fact been a heavy user of administrative resources: an addition rather than a solution to the administrator's burdens.* The point, however, is not primarily that the record, for all its interest, has been disappointing, but that it is important to understand why *it cannot in fact provide a solution for development administration at all. The bureaucratic administration, I have argued, is committed not to output but to institutional maintenance*, p. 203. (My emphasis.)

52. Mason, Horace, op.cit., p. 14.
53. du Sautoy, P., op.cit., p. 39.
    Erasmus, Charles, *Man Takes Control: Cultural Development and American Aid*, (University of Minnesota Press, 1961). On page 94, the author tells of a story of another road that was built, supposedly through "voluntary, cooperative labour". But, as it turned out, the local priest who was the project leader, used this project for his own personal advancement: "... The priest was eager to build the road in order to win approval from his superiors because he hated the cold, isolated village of Tota and was hoping to win a better parish in a milder climate. Thus the men of the poor families of Tota actually built the road while members of the upper class citizenry supervised the work."
54. Hill, Polly, *Studies in Rural Capitalism in West Africa* (Cambridge, 1970) p. 28.
55. Eldersveld, S. J., Jagannadham, V., Barnabas, A. P., *The Citizen and the Public Administrator in a Developing Democracy* (Scott, Foresman and Company, Illinois, 1968).
56. Ibid., op.cit., p. 126.
57. Ibid., op.cit., p. 23.
58. Ibid., op.cit., p. 127.
59. Szentes, Tamás, *The Political Economy of Underdevelopment* (Akadémiai Kiadó, Budapest, 1971) pp. 50—55.
60. Cama, K. H., op.cit., p. 29.
61. *UN Series Number 21*, op.cit., p. 50. This document cites, on page 66, yet another example in which the removal of colonial stumbling blocks resulted in the immediate and successful resumption of responsibilities by indigenous communities under their own leadership. The document concludes that

> ... As soon as the Ngwa Education Committee took over the literacy campaign together with their own organizer, the centers began to multiply ... There was no argument as to payment of teachers simply because each center committee and the class themselves settled their own problems. The organizer went around training instructors and assisting with supplies ... The whole campaign costs virtually nothing.

The Ngwa Education Committee was established in the town of Aba in Eastern Nigeria.

62. Ponsioen, J. A., op.cit., p. 61.
63. Erasmus, Charles, op.cit., p. 312.
64. Eldersveld, S. J., et al., op.cit., p. 8.
65. Wertheim, W. F., *East-West Parallels: Sociological Approaches to Modern Asia* (W. van Hoeve, The Hague, 1964) p. 262.
66. Szentes, Tamás, *The Structure of Society and its Change in the African Countries* (Studies on Developing Countries No. 76, Budapest, 1975) p. 33.
67. Ibid., op.cit., p. 32.
    van Velzen, Thoden, "Staff, Kulaks and Peasants: A Study of a Political Field", in *Socialism in Tanzania, Vol. 2: Policies*, edited by Lionel Cliffe and John S. Soul (East African Publishing House, 1973), pp. 153—179.
68. Wertheim, W. F., *Evolution and Revolution: Rising Waves of Emancipation.* (Penguin Books, 1974) p. 271.
69. Norman, D. W., "Economic and Non-economic Variables in Village Surveys", in *Rural Africana: A Research Bulletin of the African Studies Center, No. 8* (Michigan State University, Spring, 1968).
70. Ibid., op.cit., p. 20.
    McC. Netting, R., *Hill Farmers of Nigeria: Cultural Ecology of the Kofyar of the Jos Plateau* (University of Washington, 1968). On page 64, Robert McC. Netting gives a calender showing the farming activities of the Kofyar as well as the type of crops and techniques used. This calendar confirms that indeed, May and June are very busy months for planting of food crops in which family labour is completely occupied.
71. Magdoff, Harry, "The Impact of U.S. Foreign Policy on Underdeveloped Countries", in *Monthly Review, Vol. 22, No. 10*, March 1971, pp. 5—6.
72. Szentes, T., *The Structure of Society . . .*, op.cit., pp. 31—34.
    Stavenhagen, R., op.cit., p. 93. The author writes, on the same page:
    > Community development, it might be argued, is a *prise de conscience*, a reaction to the increasing underdevelopment of the rural community in agrarian societies. Though the notion has not been clearly defined and includes everything from primary school education to agricultural extension and medical care, the underlying assumption is that many of the problems besetting the rural populations in underdeveloped countries can be solved at the community level, with community resources and with outside intervention limited to education and technical aid. (Emphasis in the original.)
73. Erasmus, C. J., "Community Development: Science or Ideology", in *Human Organization, Vol. 27, Spring 1968, No. 1*, p. 66.
74. Ibid., op.cit., p. 66.
75. Ibid., op.cit., p. 72.
76. Frank, A. G., *Latin America: Revolution or Underdevelopment* (Monthly Review Press, 1969), pp. 248—266.
77. Ibid., op. cit., p. 262.

IV Class and Class Struggle

The past twenty and more years have seen an increasing attention being paid to the study of the concepts of "ruling élite" and "ruling class" in the independent states of Africa by social scientists. This is one of the most crucial subjects whose comprehension is a precondition to a better understanding of the socio-economic problems of these countries, especially the contribution of the internal social system to these problems.[1]

In the course of these academic debates, two schools of thought, representing almost diametrically opposed standpoints, have emerged: What might be called the conservative or liberal school, applying the concept of social *stratification and ruling élite*, argues that because contemporary Africa is not characterized by classes, the concept of class analysis is inapplicable to the study of Africa. And, on the other hand, the Marxist or radical school argues that contemporary African societies are not only characterized by a high degree of class formation, but the only relevant approach to the study of African societies is through *class analysis*. The degree of polarization between the two schools about the nature of contemporary African society and the appropriate methods for its study has been remarked upon by Robin Cohen:

In regard to literature on class in Africa, one cannot but be impressed by the number of categorial sentiments expressed on the basis of little or no empirical work. Classes are said to exist, or not to exist, almost as if their presence or absence vanished at the whim of the researcher.[2]

In this exercise, I hope to contribute to the on-going debate by supporting the view that class analysis is not only relevant and valid, but that for the real comprehension of Africa's socio-economic problems, there is no alternative to class analysis. However, class analysis in the African context, must be applied *creatively*, and, as we have repeatedly emphasized in the introduction to this paper, *local nuances must be fully taken into account* in any generalized study of African societies.

This analysis will show, among other things, that the concept of *ruling élite*, now increasingly being applied to the study of African societies, was originally intended to discredit, refute and replace the Marxist theory of class and class conflict in 18th century Europe. In this way, we draw attention to the fact that an acceptance of the ruling élite thesis would mean an acceptance of the original aims, objectives and purposes of this thesis. It is hardly necessary to point to the dire consequences for African development and change which would follow such a relegation of social responsibility on the part of radical scholarship.

69

Historical Background

It is necessary first, to trace even if only briefly, the theory of ruling élite to its historical roots in order to have a clearer understanding as to why many established social scientists writing about Africa today reject class analysis in preference to the ruling élite approach:

Gaetano Mosca, Vifredo Pareto and Robert Michels, "the élitist triad", according to James Meisel, were the first formulators of the theory of élite in 19th century Europe where the "doctrine of rule by an élite of superior individuals" was in vogue.[3] In that historical context the concept of élite represented attempts to revive some of the notions about power relations pertaining to the feudal period that had been superseded by bourgeois democratic institutions. The formulation of the theory of élite was necessitated, therefore, in the first place, by the desire in sections of the society, to revive feudal notions of social hierarchy in an attempt to arrest the new ideas of democracy: the theory of élite was antagonistic to democracy because it postulated that in every society only a minority rules, and this is contrary to the notion of majority rule (at least in theory), under democracy.[4] In the second place, élite theory was conceived as a weapon against socialism, and Marxist socialism in particular.

In time a reinterpretation of the concept of élite was made by some of its exponents in an attempt to reconcile the contradictions just indicated above. Of these theorists, Karl Mannheim and Joseph A. Schumpeter were foremost. According to Meisel,

Karl Mannheim, who perfected and refined the theory of the élite (and pointed out the self-defeating tendencies of the élitist process), also fell victim to the normative infection. Starting with a concept (his *Sociology of Knowledge*) which logically should yield a Thrasymachean view of society as a battle-field of ideologies all equally transparent and epiphenomenal to the observing social scientist, he ends up with the theory of an enlightened ruling class and social scientists whose task would be to integrate and reconcile the various clashing interests according to Right Reason ...[5]

In reference to the democratic process, Mannheim is saying that although "... the actual shaping of policy is in the hands of an élite, ... this does not mean to say that the society is not democratic. For it is sufficient for democracy that the individual citizens, though prevented from taking a direct part in government all the time, have at least the possibility of making their aspirations felt at certain intervals."[6] (See pp. 27—28 above.)

And Joseph Schumpeter could not agree more, since to him the democratic method is

That institutional arrangement for arriving at political decisions in which individuals acquire the power to decide by means of a competitive struggle for the people's vote, ...

So democracy, according to Schumpeter, "does not and cannot mean that the people actually rule in any obvious sense of the terms 'people' and 'rule'". It only means they have the right to accept or reject the men who are to rule them. 'But since they might decide this also in entirely undemocratic ways, we have ... to narrow the definition by adding a further criterion identifying the democratic method, viz., free competition among would-be leaders for the vote of the electorate'.[7]

Schumpeter means, in other words, that under a democratic political system, opportunities exist, at least in principle, for all to compete for positions of power and influence, but that majority rule in terms of more direct participation by the masses, was a practical impossibility.

It is important to note that in its classical formulations the theory of élite made no attempt to deny that society was composed of antagonistic classes based on contradictory class interests. The relevance of this remark will become clear when we discuss the theory of élite in its African context. The fact has often been pointed out that the formulations of both Mosca and Pareto exhibit close resemblance to Marx's theory of class and class conflict, and this means, among other things, that their determination and attempts to prevent the development and spread of Marxism was based on the acknowledged fact that Marx's conception of class and class struggle was "profoundly true".[8]

And, adopting the two-class scheme of Marx, both Mosca and Pareto went on to assert and stress that the minority which always ruled was efficiently *organized* in contrast to the ruled majority which was *disorganized*.[9] According to Meisel, Pareto was unconstrained in his praise for Marx:

In his COURS at any rate, he still shows a marked sympathy with Marxist view points. 'The socialist', he says, 'are entirely right to attribute great importance to the class struggle, and to call it the great factor dominating history. In that respect Karl Marx and A. Loria merit out utmost attention'. Two forms of class struggle must be distinguished. One is simply economic competition. The other operates through extra-economic channels, each class trying to secure control of the government to use it as 'a machine of spoliation'. Pareto is outmarxing Marx when he proclaims that 'the struggle in the course of which some individuals appropriate the wealth produced by others is the great fact dominating all human history. *It is disguised and disappears behind the most various pretexts which have often misled the historians.* One might even say that it is only in our time that the full truth has become known.'[10] (My emphasis.)

It is also important to note that the classical élite theorists justified both minority rule and existing class divisions—with the consequent social inequalities—all of which they saw as *natural* and *inevitable*. Meisel declares:

Elitism—at its crudest the notion that The Few should rule because they do in fact rule, and less crudely the contention that, since only a few can rule, The Many do not and never will...

Although

... It is also true that history is the graveyard of aristocracies, *but from that graveyard arise, phoenix-like, forever new élite formations to eternalize the cycle of domination.* No matter whether the economy remains capitalistic or becomes the plaything of equalitarian levelers, *there will always be a ruling class, and therefore exploitation.*[11] (My emphasis.)

71

There was no attempt either, by the classical élite theorists, to disguise or conceal their anti-Marxism and their determination to eliminate Marxist socialism from the face of the earth. According to Mosca, one of the best methods to achieve this objective was through the creation of a new social science, because

In the world in which we are living socialism will be arrested only if a realistic political science succeeds in demolishing the metaphysical and optimistic methods that prevail at present in social studies . . .[12]

When Mosca came to consider the various alternative methods open to him to-wards the practical solutions of the problems of domination, of conflict and exploitation implicit in élitism, he rejected both socialism and liberal laissez faire, and placed his hopes, as Mannheim was do later, on rule by "merit" or "virtue". The "realistic" social science, he imagined hopefully, would lead to the creation of a social group whose qualities would be based on their educational achievements and superiority. Because, Mosca argued,

If there is any social class prepared to set aside, if only for a while, the private interests, and able to perceive the common good with the detachment needed, it is certainly the one which, thanks to its exacting intellectual training, has what should make for nobility of character, for broad horizons and for enlarged faculties . . . of foresight and prevention: that class, and that class alone will freely sacrifice a present good in order to avert a future evil.[13]

Out of this crystal ball-gazing come intimations from Mosca that the whole structure of society will increasingly become more "open", thus permitting ever increasing numbers of those who have availed themselves of the educational opportunities to enter the circles of the ruling classes. According to Mosca, this will ensure, among other things, that no single class will become permanent-ly entrenched within the social structure on the basis of its monopoly of political power and wealth.[14]

I hope that this brief outline of the historical origins of the theory of élite has brought out some of the main elements of that theory, and thus providing us with the necessary background upon which the application of this theory to African studies can be better comprehended.

Elite Theory: Its Introduction and Application to Africa

The introduction of the theory of élite and its application to the study of Africa came, similarly, with what Gunnar Myrdal has described graphically as the "swelling flood of research" from Western capitalist countries after the Second World War.[15]

The studies of African élites started with the publications of J. E. Goldthorpe and others in the 1950's.[16] These were followed by the studies of such writers as S. F. Nadel, P. C. Lloyd and others. Lloyd has written extensively and more consistently on the subject of élite and their social role in his studies of West Africa, which, although mainly centered in Nigeria, are assumed by the author to have general application or validity throughout tropical Africa.[17] It is for this reason that in this paper Lloyd's analysis is given special attention. His studies are also thought to be a fair representation of liberal or conservative theories which are the target of our criticism.

STRUCTURE OF SOCIETY

Lloyd sees contemporary African society as being divided into two main parts —the *élite* and the *masses*. The élite is further subdivided into the "élite proper", and a "marginal sub-élite" and an "earlier traditional élite". The masses are composed of three main sub-groupings of *urban workers, migrant workers* and a *rural peasantry*. Lloyd, however, sees the main line of demarcation as lying between the élite and the masses.[18]

In this respect, Lloyd's concept of African societies closely resemble those of Mosca and Pareto, and especially Pareto's élite—nonélite dichotomy. However, Lloyd does not make any direct reference in any of his writings that I have seen so far, to the works of the classical masters of the theory of élite. Lloyd's theory of African élites unfolds as he proceeds to describe in detail the various groups into which he has divided African society—their composition, group characteristics, relationship to each other, and the respective roles which each group is supposed to play in African development and change. When the groups are examined, each in turn, the following picture emerges:

ÉLITES AND THEIR COMPOSITION

Lloyd defines the "modern" African élite simply as "those persons who were Western educated and wealthy to a high degree relative to the masses of the population".[19] Possession of Western education and wealth are, therefore, the major criteria distinguishing the élite from the masses: the élite are in their position of privilege because of their monopoly of these all essential attributes which the masses totally lack, or else do not posses these attributes in their "correct proportion". The élite is a "Westernized" group whose symbols of wealth and style of life are Western.[20]

The definition of élite receives further clarification in the following passage in which Lloyd also makes a distinction between the "élite proper" and the other élites. He states that

Excluded by definition are the wealthy but illiterate or semiliterate traders, traditionally orientated and often prominent within their town of birth. Marginal to the group are the educated obas and chiefs, men of affluence but slight influence outside their towns. The élites are thus the bureaucrats, the secondary school teachers and university lecturers, and the politicians.[21]

Lloyd is aware of the fact that by defining his élites in this manner, he consequently underrates the power and influence of the traditional rulers in tropical Africa. He tries to correct this mistake by saying that

It should be appreciated that through their close contact with the masses, both the marginal élite and the sub-élite may, in some contexts, be more significant as reference groups to the masses than are the élites of our present definition.[22]

But despite this acknowledgement, Lloyd remains ambivalent, to say the least, in his attitude towards the position of these two élite groups. The reason for this is, however, not too difficult to find: Lloyd, as we shall see later, is so committed to this "modernizing", Western educated élite, that all the other groups in society—traditional rulers, workers, peasants and so forth—all come to be viewed as "marginal" or mere spectators on the political scene by him.[23]

Contrary to Lloyd's views, there is abundant evidence to demonstrate the important role played by these two groups during and after colonial rule. Incidentaly some of this evidence is provided by Lloyd himself whe he correctly points out, for example, that where chieftaincy was abolished, as in French-speaking Guinea in 1958, those "able office-holders loyal to the Parti Démocratique de Guinée (P.D.G.), were absorbed into other administrative posts". However, he fails to draw the correct conclusion from this, which is that these traditional rulers thus became an integral part of the ruling class.[24]

Martin Kilson, among others, has demonstrated that the colonial situation had the effect of both weakening and bolstering the authority of traditional rulers. The extent to which these effects occurred, depended, of course, on the particular circumstances of the territory in question. This correct assessment enables Kilson to arrive at the right conclusion, which is that

... In the period of nationalist political change one can expect to find traditional rulers shifting, *especially as the central political power shifts, slowly but definitely away from accommodation to colonial rule toward a shrewd selection of political allies among competing nationalist groups.* Again, this shifting will be governed by the chief's calculation of which nationalist group will best enable them to maximize modern resources of power and simultaneously retain much of their traditional authority.[25] (My emphasis.)

It is important to have a clear grasp of these factors because, as it will be shown later, they have a significant bearing on the class analysis of African societies.

S. F. Nadel, as I have already indicated, is among those who have played a leading role in the exportation of the concept of élite to Africa and other parts of the underdeveloped world in the early 1950s. The influence of Nadel's approach on the subject of élite is most evident in the writings of P. C. Lloyd: Writing in 1956, Nadel singled out one factor which he thought most clearly distinguished that group which deserved to be called an élite, and this is "imitability". The élite, Nadel said,

... is looked up to, and imitated, because it is credited with important gifts and desirable attributes. Thus the élite, by its very manner of acting and thinking, sets the standards for the whole society, its influence and power being that of a model accepted and considered worth following.[26]

And Lloyd, writing in 1966, describes how Western ideas and values assimilated by the Western educated élite are then transmitted to their supposedly admiring masses in the following way:

... The élite influences the behaviour of the masses; it is an imitable body of persons. *Influence is here distinguished from power and authority.* The latter are associated with institutionalized relationships and structures, the former with non-structured relationships and with informal networks of communication.[27] (My emphasis.)

Gavin N. Kitching has recently pointed out the important fact that Nadel's analysis marks the shift of focus away from the analysis of the classical writers, notably, Gaetano Mosca and Vilfredo Pareto. This shift expresses a deliberate attempt on the part of Nadel, Lloyd and others, to *emasculate* the concept of élite of its *political content*.[28] More about this later.

Composition. Lloyd sees the African élite as a small, homogeneous and cohesive group with a similar background: they come from a humble social background and they still maintain links with their village and kin, although they are "Westernized". They reside in the national or regional capitals where they share the same sulubrious residences afforded them by their high salaries. They share a common educational experience and they belong to the same formal organizations such as the Rotary Club, Old Boys Associations, but they simultaneously take part in the activities and the affairs of their village or town ethnic associations. According to Lloyd, it is all these desirable attributes which enable the African élite to serve as a model for the masses.[29]

However, it must not be assumed from this, Lloyd tells us, that intra-élite relationships are always or necessarily characterized by harmony and friendship. On the contrary, intra-élite conflicts are quite common:

... Although the members of the élite of an African nation tend to have common social background and educational experience, rivalry for power occurs between politicians, civil servants, army officers, each stressing the legitimacy of those criteria—popular support, educational qualifications, force—which favour itself.[30]

Although "power" is mentioned as a component of intra-élite rivalry in this passage, Lloyd stresses in all his writings that the nature of this conflict within the élite must be understood in terms of competition for occupational roles within an "open" stratification system. Such conflicts, therefore, are engaged into, in accordance with established norms, and thus their resolution is reached, generally speaking, through the available "institutionalized channels". In other words, to the extent that the intra-élite conflicts have any political content which go beyond the "friendly" competition for occupational roles, such conflicts are motivated by the need, on the part of the élite, to demonstrate to the outside world that political control, in the given country, is based on democratic practices. Thus the élites, in accordance with the manner in which democracy

75

has been defined (page 70 above), engage in competition at intervals, for the vote of the electorate.[31] Lloyd makes this point very clear when he states that

A governing élite tends to be a more highly corporate group. Yet it may *lack the components of innovation and imitability. It may even be viewed with hostility by other élite groups or by the masses, and in these circumstances the designation of élite would seem to be inappropriate.*[32] (My emphasis.)

A similar view has been expressed previously by Nadel, but the other way round. However, the meaning remains the same, namely that a true élite should remain "pure" or untainted by the political brush because, as Nadel declares, this group ". . . is first and foremost a ruling group, and only incidentally an élite . . . The class of people holding or sharing political power, as we all know, may well be hostile to the ideals and values embodied in the other élites, e.g. being anti-intellectual or anti-capitalist or whatever the case may be. More important, the governing group may have no standards of its own to contribute which would be acceptable to the rest of the people."[33]

The Masses

Both Mosca and Pareto saw the masses, "the ruled majority" (Mosca) or the "non-élite" (Pareto), as mere objects subject to manipulation by the élite but never a party to any political decision making.[34] As Kitching correctly points out, "classical élite theory was used primarily to explain why the powerless masses will always remain so, even if they seek to alter their exploited position vis-a-vis the élite by joining together in organizations".[35] This is *exactly the way* Lloyd views the African masses, who, in contrast to his Western educated élite, seem utterly incapable of organizing themselves into any effective opposition against any force that oppresses them.[36] This becomes crystal clear when we examine the three groups, each in turn, into which Lloyd has divided the African masses.

i) *Urban workers*

This, according to Lloyd, is a generally poverty-stricken group found in the slums of African towns. Although they dwell in the "right" cultural environment (urban Western values etc.,) these workers prefer membership and participation in their own ethnic associations per se. While admitting that these associations have some positive role to play, in that for example, they facilitate the worker's entry into the unfamiliar urban surroundings and so on, they are generally seen as acting to hinder or prevent the worker from making a clean break with his traditional values, a precondition without which, it is implied, these workers can never hope to compete successfully for employment opportunities being offered in the towns.

This being the case, Lloyd argues, it would be unrealistic for anyone to expect any revolutionary potential from such a group, encapsulated, as it is still, in primordial activities, and completely lacking in any class consciousness. So deep-rooted are these manifestations in the African workers that even when they resort to violence, as they do from time to time, it has been shown that in fact these outbursts have little to do, if at all, with the question of occupational strata or class struggle; these violent outbursts, Lloyd concludes, are based on *tribal* hostility which is so deep-seated in the African.[37]

ii) *Migrant workers*

This category of workers (further subdivided into seasonal, short-staying and long-staying) comes to the towns only for short periods and for specific purposes, namely to earn some cash with which to purchase such consumer goods (for status symbols) as bicycles, sewing machines etc. This is the group generally referred to by social anthropologists and sociologists as "target" workers. These workers are supposed to have *limited needs and simple tastes* that are easily satisfied. Lloyd argues that although a new range of opportunities are open to the towns, this group is hindered and constrained from taking full advantage of these opportunities because of several factors:

For example, the migrants lack educational qualifications; they have no personal contacts, and even more important in Lloyd's view, is the migrants' general failure to cast off much of their allegiance to the village and adopt new urban values. In this particular respect, according to Lloyd, the migrants are even worse off than the urban workers because the attachment to the village and its primordial sentiments are much stronger in the migrants. And, as in the case of urban workers, the migrants naturally join their ethnic associations in the towns— associations which, as we have been told already, allegedly act to perpetuate these primordial sentiments and behaviour.[38]

Lloyd then proceeds to identify various factors which are supposed to explain why migrants leave the rural areas for the towns: these include pressure of population on the land, lack of employment opportunities, and changes in the ownership of land as a result of which communal ownership is being replaced by private ownership of land. And, as a further consequence of the latter, there has been growing emphasis on the production of cash crops for export rather than food crops. It is important here, to note that of all these factors, Lloyd chooses to emphasize that it is the availability of new opportunities in the towns which pulls the migrants away from the rural areas:

We stress the lack of opportunities in the rural areas. And so we must emphasize, too, that the migrants are not often from the lowest rural social stratum, forced to emigrate because their lands have been expropriated. They are men who probably have more initiative than their neighbours, and who are prepared to face the risks attendant upon migration in order to strive for economic success and a style of life that is not possible in the rural areas.[39]

In choosing to stress the supposed availability of new opportunities as the primary factor which compels the migrants to move to the towns, Lloyd is not only upholding the values of capitalism, but he is deliberately trying to de-emphasize and conceal those aspects of migration whose deeper examination would reveal the true nature of the *process* of capitalist underdevelopment and all its attendant relations of exploitation. We shall expand on this shortly.

iii) *Rural Peasantry*

Lloyd sees this subgroup simply as an amorphous mass. However, he "rejects" as "simplistic" some of the common assumptions by which peasants have been characterized by social scientists. These characteristics, which are viewed in negative terms as being inhibitory to social change and economic development, assert, among other things: that peasants subordinate their personal aims to those of the family; that there is lack of cooperation among peasant communities because of mutual distrust; that peasants have simple or limited aspirations and needs; that they lack any sense of deferred gratification; that they are fatalistic about the world to which they have a very narrow view; that they are tradition-bound and lack the innovating spirit, and finally, that they show both dependency and hostility on and towards authority and government.[40]

Lloyd is able to show that although the peasantry is the group that contributes most to the creation of national wealth, its own share of this wealth is abysmally small. These and many other remarks and observations by Lloyd, show that he clearly sees the peasantry as an economically exploited group in society, a group with a magnitude of grievances as a direct result of this exploitation.[41] Lloyd warns, however, that it would be a mistake to expect that peasants have the ability to redress their grievances: Although peasant revolts often occur, he claims, it has been shown that peasants are unable to sustain these rebellions which, at any rate, are never clearly comprehended and articulated. Thus having "rejected" as simplistic, the received theories and views on the characteristics of peasants and peasant societies, Lloyd seems to end in full agreement with those same assumptions when he states that "hence peasants are merely passive spectators of political struggles, or else they long for the advent of a millenium, without specifying for themselves and their neighbours the rungs on the staircase to heaven."[42]

Lloyd expresses his full conviction about the lack of any potential on the part of the peasantry to engage in sustained political struggle when he confidently concludes that

Their leaders, in power today, are far more influenced by pressures from the urban élite and by strike threats from the workers than mumblings of discontent in the villages.[43]

The attempted summary of Lloyd's analysis of African rural populations has been made largely without much critical comment. We now proceed to chal-

78

lenge his views, especially in reference to migrant workers and the alleged absence of class divisions in rural Africa.

In his *Social Classes in Agrarian Societies*,[44] Rodolfo Stavenhagen has devoted several chapters to the analysis of rural African social structures. In his analysis he identifies three main social categories and shows why these groups should be considered either to be *social classes* or mere *social categories*:

1. *Seasonal Migrant Workers:* this, according to Stavenhagen, is a *transitional* category which does not constitute a class by itself. However, the fact that this social category participates in a money economy, means that it thereby achieves a class character. Furthermore, it is actually the maintenance of a subsistence economy which prevents this group from becoming a full-fledged social class. Stavenhagen suggests, therefore, that the migrant worker must be seen as a new type of peasant who is tied to the development of agricultural capitalism in various parts of rural Africa. More about this group later.[45]

2. *Agricultural labourers:* this is a group employed in commercial plantations which produce cash crops. It is, according to Stavenhagen, an *emergent class* which seems to be developing rapidly in some of the states (as we shall see) of tropical Africa.[46]

3. *Commercial Farmers:* this group is *a class* which, because of its relative prosperity, *employs the labour of others*, especially immigrant workers who are generally grossly under-paid. This class, according to Stavenhagen, is itself internally differentiated, and he illustrates this point by showing that among the Yoruba of Western Nigeria, where this differentiation is very marked,

Almost half of the farmers produce less than 10 percent of the total cocoa crop, while 15 percent of the farmers produce more than half of the total crop. Moreover, the members of the old and dominant class, the warrior nobility and the aristocracy, own the largest plantations and receive the highest incomes.[47]

These observations tie in with those of Fitch and Oppenheimer in reference to cocoa farmers in Ghana. We quote their remarks at legnth because they are significant:

Another widespread myth about Ghanaian cocoa production is that cocoa is farmed by independent smallholders. Polly Hill calls this 'the myth of the peasant farmer, who, though unfamiliar with the cash economy, nonetheless succeeded in the space of twenty years in transforming the economy of Ghana'. The mythology specifies that this peasant farmer has only a small amount of land—one to two acres—and does all his work himself. But while the heterogeneity of the social organization of cocoa farming in Ghana almost defies generalization, it is clear that in both Ashanti and Southern Ghana the cocoa landowner is an employer of labor. Polly Hill's field investigations throughout Ghana showed that the proportion of independent smallholders (those who perform all their own labor) is probably less than 20 percent of the total.

That section of the owning class which is distinguished by its ability to employ labor can itself be broken down into two strata: the capitalist farmers who have been able to accumulate enough capital to set themselves up as creditors; and the small farmers who have fallen into debt and pledged their land.[48]

In reference to income differentials within the farming community in Ghana, recent evidence "... clearly reveals the development of a class of extremely large, wealthy farmers some of whom earn as much as NC. 12,000 per annum." The following table illustrates this claim:[49]

Table 1

Income Class, NC.	Percentage of farmers	Total Income, NC.M.
1— 60	18.0	1.7
60— 120	20.0	4.2
120— 240	22.0	9.1
240— 600	25.0	22.2
600—1200	10.0	19.1
1200 and above	5.0	25.7

NB. Not including imputed income from consumption of own food.

Source: Kodwo Ewusi, The Distribution of Monetary Incomes in Ghana (Legon: ISSER, 1971), p. 75.

We must now return to Stavenhagen and his analysis of the process of migration and some of its effects and consequences. Migration, according to Stavenhagen, are of two main types:

1. Migration to the mining, industrial and urban centers of Southern Africa —the Copper Belt of Zambia, the mining towns of Zaire, Rhodesia and the Republic of South Africa. This type of migration, according to Stavenhagen, leads to the formation of an industrial proletariat, whose size or strength varies from one country to another.[50]

2. Migrations to commercial agricultural regions. These mainly occur in East and West Africa, and in this case, there is a tendency for the emergence and development of a rural proletariat, as shown below.

Stavenhagen suggests several reasons as explanation for the fact that these migrants do not undergo a full transformation but retain much of their traditional ties and the so-called primordial values. For example, taking the problem of so-called "target workers", Stavenhagen shows, and convincingly too, that the real reason why these migrants only remain in their work places for limited periods is because

The capitalist system needs to preserve the old system of subsistence agriculture, and the social structures associated with it: However, the very demands of capitalist development tend to destroy these.[51]

These capitalist needs for preserving the pre-capitalist modes of production and other vestiges of the old society, find their expression in the labour policies of governments and the commercial companies concerned:

> The mining companies and the administration have done everything possible to assure that the worker returns to his reserve as soon as he fulfils the terms of his contract. It was always in the interests of the colonial administration and the mining companies that the migratory worker preserves his ties to his own community and its agricultural activities.[52]

To show how the agricultural working class is emerging, Stavenhagen gives two examples from West Africa:

1. *Liberia:* Stavenhagen shows that under the American company, Firestone, while some plantation workers are still employed on a seasonal basis, the majority of the workers are now on a permanent, stable, salaried basis. The majority of this labour force is unskilled and paid on a piece work basis, but nevertheless, their work is carried out under strict discipline and organizational framework. When this labour force is seen, as it must, from "the hierarchical nature of Liberian society (with its Americanized bourgeoisie almost totally detached from the rest of the population) provides the objective conditions for the spread of class consciousness". Stavenhagen points out significantly that there is in fact a potential influence for the development of this class consciousness in view of the fact that these workers are in contact with nationalist movements from neighbouring countries such as Guinea-Bissau.[53]

2. In the *Republic of the Cameroon,* which is the second example given by Stavenhagen, the Development Corporation, a government agency, administers the plantations on which cash crops such as bananas, palmoil, cocoa and rubber are produced. Here also

> ... The majority of the workers are unskilled. The organization of the work is virtually the same as on the Liberian plantations. Wages are paid monthly on the basis of days worked, and the work week is 45 hours, divided over 6 days.
> ... Immigrant workers, especially those who are accompanied by their faimlies *attempt to establish themselves permanently in the plantation region.*[54] (My emphasis.)

To Stavenhagen then, this stable and salaried agricultural labour force, working under the most rigorously organized and disciplined conditions, constitutes a *rural working class.* Admittedly, this class is in its early stages of formation, but this fact does not, and cannot be used, as an argument against its existence.

The exposition of the theory of élite in the preceding pages provides us with the necessary background upon which the protagonists of the élite theory base their objections to the use or application of class analysis in the study of contemporary African societies. The following pages will show further, how the exponents of the stratification-élite theories have modified and distorted the very concept of élite in order to offer it as a "valid" alternative to class analysis.[55]

In his discussion as to how these modifications and distortions in the élite theory have been perpetrated, Gavin Kitching goes to the heart of the matter when he declares that

... In short, the central objection to the use of the concept of class in tropical Africa depends on a tacit acceptance of the *supposedly Marxist view, that classes must be in class conflict, produced by class consciousness before this form of analysis can be of use.*[56] (My emphasis.)

It is from this rigid and erroneous interpretation of Marx's concept of class and its integral aspects of class struggle and class consciousness that the exponents of élite theory proceed to argue that the alleged absence of class struggle and class consciousness must be taken as "proof" that there are no social classes in African societies. Therefore, so the argument is concluded, class analysis is irrelevant or cannot be used in the study of Africa.

Social class

As it is well-known, Marx died before he could complete the formulation, definition and elaboration of the concept of class and this has created great problems in later attempts to analyse and apply this concept. Various parts of Marx's initial formulation of the concept of class are to be found scattered in various parts of his works. For example, in *Capital Volume III*, Marx distinguishes three main classes:

The owners of merely labour power, owners of capital and land-owners, whose respective sources of income are wages, profit and ground-rent, in other words, wage labourers, capitalists and land-owners constitute the three big classes of modern society based upon the capitalist mode of production.[57]

In *The Eighteenth Brumaire of Louis Bonaparte*, Marx defines the concept of class under a *concrete historical* setting:

Thus a great mass of the French nation is formed by the simple addition of isomorphous magnitudes, much as potatoes in a sack form a sack of potatoes. Insofar as millions of families live under economic conditions of existence that separate their mode of life, their interests and cultural formation *from those of the other classes and bring them into conflict with those classes, they form a class.* Insofar as these small peasant proprietors are *merely connected on a local basis and the identity of their interests fails to produce a feeling of community, national links, or a political organization, they do not form a class. They are therefore incapable of asserting their class interest in their own name,* whether through a parliament or through a convention.[58] (My emphasis.)

Although some of the writers in the liberal school concede that a "rudimentary" or "incipient" class has already emerged in tropical Africa, the general view held from this quarter is that the notion of class is foreign and alien to Black Africa. While Lloyd concedes, for instance, that there are grounds for calling the African *élite* a "class", he maintains that this does not suggest the existence of a class system as such:

Furthermore, while the élite has the cohesion, the consciousness of privilege and distinct styles of life to merit the term class, it is not balanced by another recognisable class—unless one restricts one's use of such terminology to the modern sector, and terms the urban manual workers an incipient class.[59]

Lloyd proceeds to argue that no class system can be expected to develop within a social structure which remains "open", allowing members of society to compete freely for positions of power, privilege and prestige. African societies, both traditional and contemporary, are, according to this argument, "open", although they are not to be regarded as "perfect" since individuals do not necessarily stand an equal chance of success in the competition for these positions.[60]

Lloyd goes on to conclude that in fact no other group, apart from the élite, does deserve the term class, and he tries to show why this must be so:

Finally, a social class can only exist in a system of classes. There can be no upper class without a lower class. In their homogeneity, hereditary characteristics and class consciousness, the classes should resemble one another. But if the African élite forms an upper class, where are the lower classes? The peasantry still thinks in terms of ethnic units, with descent and age as the main criteria of stratification and social divisions. The sub-élite of clerks, primary school teachers, and skilled artisans are perhaps slightly less ethnically oriented, but actively aspire to élite membership. The urban labourer remains ethnically oriented, often relying on his ethnic association for his social security.[61]

Gavin Kitching clarifies this statement when he shows that those who argue against the use of class analysis in Africa "consider that although it might be possible to regard the top-most stratum of politicians, military and bureaucrats in these states as a Ruling Class since they have political power, control of most of their nation's economic resources, and a monopoly of the means of violence, this would be unwarranted because there are no equivalent strata below this level to make up a class system or class society. Hence, it is argued, it is better to stick to the term élite."[62]

Against Lloyd's argument in reference to the "missing" classes, several writers have suggested that the upper class in tropical Africa is largely foreign, "that is, it consists of foreign companies, banks and governments who are largely responsible for generating and controlling economic development . . ."[61] Peter Waterman writes, in this connection, for example, that

In Nigeria this class is the product and mediator of foreign capitalist penetration. It is "middle" in its position between foreign exploiter and exploited mass. For its income it is totally dependent on imperialist investments of both a direct and indirect kind (salaries in the case of private employees, 'aid' and 'loans' to governmental and para-governmental institutions in the case of officialdom). Its values are determined by its work situation: divorced from productive activity makes them totally consumption oriented; complex career structures, grading and rewards encourage the ideal bureaucratic attitudes.[64]

In reference to the assertion that "a social class can only exist in a system of classes", (with which we agree) it is of interest to note that it is from some of the social stratification theorists themselves that a serious challenge against this question of class- what does mobility mean? Ultra- family differences in social class-

has come. Leonard Plotnicov, for example, has recently raised reservations against this assumption, or rather its hidden meaning and intention. He has actually gone so far as to suggest a way out of this apparently self-imposed restriction. He writes:

... We tie our hands by a circular definition—there is no social class system without classes, there are no classes without a social class system. What warrants the assumption that a social class system must appear full-blown when it emerges within a previously classless society? May we not assume, with perhaps more justification, that it develops part by part, class by class?[65]

However, this insightful questioning does not, as one would have hoped, lead Plotnicov to "self-liberation" from the received conventional wisdom: In his studies of Jos in Northern Nigeria, Plotnicov has found that there is a top class of politicians and bureaucrats, with the rest of the inhabitants consisting of an undifferentiated mass. The top class, he succumbs, is an "élite".

Another objection against the use of class analysis raised by Lloyd and others, is that it would be erroneous to assume that the system of class formations which characterized the development of European societies observed by Marx would be reproduced in tropical Africa. In issuing this warning (with which no social scientist worthy of that name would disagree), Lloyd in fact intends to say much more than that: he intends to say that the lack of similarities between Western middle classes and his African élites suggest the absence of social classes in tropical Africa. And to make this easier for himself, Lloyd only concerns himself with making superficial comparisons about individual and group attitudes and mannerism, e.g., how African élites dress, converse, interact among themselves, relate to their spouses, and how they bring up their children and so forth—in comparison with their counterparts in Western Europe.[66] In other words, these superficial and meaningless observations are based on an insufficient historical facts and evidence, as Immanuel Wallerstein shows:

Can we speak of classes in contemporary Africa? Is class conflict a fundamental or even an important explanation of African political life? For those who say no, the argument usually is based on the fact that some classes are largely 'missing' in Africa, or that 'ethnic' or other interpersonal links are far more determinative of political actions than class membership. Usually the negative position is couched, explicitly or implicitly, in a comparative frame: i.e., while 'class' may be said to matter in Europe, it does not in Africa. This negative view, often expressed very cavalierly, seems to me to misread simultaneously the contemporary African scene, the real history of Western Europe, and the arguments of classical Marxist class analysis.[67]

Recent publications by social scientists who base their research on concrete historical evidence enable us to discover how the present social formations in Africa have evolved through history. These writers are in a position to show therefore, not only that the Western model has not been reproduced in Africa, but also some of the main reasons why. Even more important is the fact that these writers are able to demonstrate the types of social formations, taking full account of local nuances, which have emerged and continue to crystallize in tropical Africa. Through their analysis we also come to perceive how the African ruling classes differ substantially from their counterparts in Western Europe.[68] For example, Walter Rodney shows why the Western model of class formation was not reproduced, at least not in its exact form, through the process of colonization:

Capitalism as a system within the metropoles or epicenters had two dominant classes: Firstly, the capitalists or bourgeoisie who owned the factories and banks (the major means of production and distribution of wealth); and secondly, the workers or proletariat who worked in the factories of the said bourgeoisie. Colonialism did not create a capital-owning and factory-owning class among Africans or even inside Africa; nor did it create any urbanized proletariat of any significance (particularly outside of South Africa). In other words, capitalism in the form of colonialism failed to perform in Africa the task which it performed in Europe in changing social relations and liberating the forces of production.[69]

However, capitalism helped to accellerate the process of decomposition of the African communal village life, processes which had already been taking place through the emergence of empires and states, some of which date back to the 10th century—long before there was contact between Africa and Europe.[70]

In this connection, Samir Amin suggests that although social differentiation on the basis of social division of labour already existed in the African village community, such class differences that existed were not *antagonistic*. Amin concludes that almost all contemporary societies of West Africa are *class societies*, and that the ideology of *classlessness* being propagated by African ruling classes and their academic articulators is based on the superficial observation of the existence of egalitarianism in African societies, both traditional and contemporary. Amin goes on to give a timely warning against dogmatism "of no matter what thesis", which is prevalent today in studies of class formations in Africa. Pointing out the motive behind this tendency on the part of conservative and "establishment" Marxists, Amin states that

...At times to justify a conciliatory attitude towards this or that political group in power, they will say on the contrary: 'since neither slavery nor the serf system nor wage system are dominant modes of production, our society is fundamentally a classless society', or again, to weaken the point of this affirmation in view of the future, they will say: 'among us class differences are not very sharply defined', which does not mean very much.[71]

Amin urges Marxists to assert and stress those aspects of the Marxist method of research which have a universal validity. His own studies examine how, in concrete situations in specific African countries, social formations have evolved and continue to do so. In reference to the Marxist method, Amin believes that

What has retained its universal meaning in the lesson of Marxism is its *method*, the theory of the primacy of the forces of production, explaining how these forces determine in the last analysis the dynamics of production and beyond that the framework of the societies.

Starting from here, *it is a universal truth that when human societies reach a certain degree of development of their productive forces, they break up into antagonistic social classes.*[72] (My emphasis.)

The Marxist method, which Amin correctly stresses in this passage, consists, as it is well-known, of two branches namely, Historical Materialism and Dialectical Materialism. As we have already indicated the premises upon which historical materialism operates (see page 47 above), we shall now further clarify the concept of dialectical materialism, which, as we have seen (page 46 above), was singled out for attack by de Schlippe. On the basis of that *unsupported* attack on dialectical materialism by de Schlippe, we could not even begin to have an understanding of the real nature of this concept. One of the clearest exposition of dialectical materialism is provided by Mao Tse-tung:

The Marxist philosophy of dialectical materialism has two outstanding characteristics. One is its class nature: it openly avows that dialectical materialism is in the service of the proletariat (all the oppressed). The other is its practicality: it emphasizes the dependence of theory on practice, emphasizing that theory is based on practice and in turn serves practice.[73]

We shall return to the concept of dialectical materialism later when we deal with the question of dogmatism, but here it is important to stress the fact that historical materialism and dialectical materialism are an *integral,* and therefore, *inseparable* parts of the Marxist method.

What kind of class systems have emerged when African societies reached the level of development of their productive forces which Amin refers to above? The *varied* historical, economic, political and cultural experiences of the states of tropical Africa which we have stressed from the beginning of this paper, suggest and mean that there are formidable analytical problems to overcome or at least to take into account before a comprehensive and "general" class model for Africa can be formulated. Taking all this into consideration, Gavin Kitching has attempted to formulate such a model. This attempt provides the basis upon which further formulations, based *on more concrete, historical situations*, might be fruitfully pursued. Kitching is aware of its inherent limitations, and therefore, he stresses the tentative nature of his formulations. Briefly summarised, the following picture appears from Kitching's suggested class model:[74]

1. *Ruling Class:* According to Kitching, this is a class which is

distinguished by its *Western standard of living,* founded on *high levels of education and the possession of scarce managerial and technical skills.* In some cases a part of this class owns society's means of production, but in most cases these are small-scale, and either dominated by foreign capital, or controlled by state bureaucracies. In the former case, a part of the indigenous Ruling Class merely acts as agents for foreign capital. In the latter case, a greater part of the profits of the enterprises in question remains within the state, but this may imply that this Ruling Class benefits disproportionately, vis-á-vis other strata *unless effective measures making for a more equal distribution of income are also in force.*[75] (My emphasis.)

In an attempt to further clarify his own formulation just quoted, Kitching, by way of conclusion, adds that

These Ruling Classes must be seen as internally divided, both on the basis of function (political, military, and bureaucratic personnel) and also by tribal or regional origin, though these often overlap. (Page 348.)

Kitching's conceptualization and formulation of the structure of the ruling classes in tropical Africa can be criticized on several important grounds: Firstly, by stressing "western standards of living" and monopoly of Western education and managerial skills by the ruling classes as their distinguishing characteristics, he has, wittingly or unwittingly, *reverted* to the definitions and conceptualizations of the élites by élitist theorists such as Mosca, Mannheim, Lloyd and Nadel, which have been criticized above (see pages 70, 72—76). Secondly, and perhaps partly because of the way he has formulated the structure of the ruling classes, Kitching subsequently fails to explore the relations of exploitation and domination between these classes and the oppressed classes. Instead, he seems satisfied in merely making an indirect reference to the effect that in certain cases exploitation *may* characterize the relationship between the ruling classes and the oppressed classes. He implies further, that the remedy for these relations of exploitation might be the introduction of "effective measures making for a more equal distribution of income". To accept the efficacy of such "remedies" as these, would mean that we succumb to bourgeois reformism which have little to do with the *eradication* of the root causes of social problems and the *liberation* of the oppressed classes.

Thirdly, by lumping together politicians, military, and bureaucrats, as components of the ruling class, Kitching seems to suggest that all gradations of "politicians", all echelons of the bureaucracy, and all ranks of the police force and the military, are to be regarded as the Ruling Class. Failure to make a clear distinction between the "greater" and "lesser" enemy, like the failure to identify and define correctly the problem against which the revolutionary effort is directed, will result in serious problems, for example, in the selection and recruitment of those forces which should constitute the revolutionary alliance. These weaknessess cast a shadow on Kitching's class analysis with which we are otherwise in *general agreement*.

2. *Middle Class:* Kitching suggests that this class must be viewed as being exceedingly differentiated into white-collar workers, academics, members of the free professions, middle and lower bureaucrats and school teachers, middle and lower level traders. This stratum is distinguished from the urban manual workers by its high income and non-manual status.[76]

3. *Urban Manual Workers:* Kitching subdivides this stratum into a minority of skilled workers which is highly unionized and receiving high wages relative

to the larger number of unskilled workers. This internal differentiation within this stratum has been regarded by many social scientists as a problematic for the collective bargaining and the unity of this stratum of workers vis-á-vis their employers. In the controversy which is still raging, some writers have gone so far as to claim that the skilled workers are to be viewed as a "labour aristocracy", who, in order to preserve and advance further their own position of privilege, are more likely to collaborate with management against their fellow workers—the lowly paid unskilled labourers.[77] However, others have argued against this contention, showing that such wage differentials as exist between the two groups of workers have not, perhaps in most cases, prevented joint labour action by the two groups of workers against the employer who is correctly perceived as a common enemy.[78]

4. *Peasantry:* Coming to the rural areas, Kitching identifies two main strata into which the peasantry is divided. These, according to him, are emerging classes of richer peasants and poorer peasants. The richer peasants include large landowners or producers of cash crops such as cocoa, coffee and so forth., while poorer peasants are those with smallholdings, producing for home consumption. In terms of power relations, Kitching points out that the richer peasants control local cooperative markets and have easy access to local agricultural extension officers and the ruling classes in the national or regional capitals. (See pages 57—58 above.) In some areas, Kitching shows, the poorer peasants may be tenant or debt farmers of the richer peasants, or even become agricultural recruits to the latter along with landless rural labourers and "strangers".

In showing that there is differentiation among the peasantry, Kitching refutes another of the objections against the use of class analysis, and

This is the contention that even if it is possible to isolate broad class divisions within the urban areas, it is not possible to do so in the rural hinterlands which are populated by a mass of uniformly impoverished smallholding peasants. Since this group constitutes 80 percent or more of the population in most new African states, its very existence it is argued, makes it meaningless to speak of these states as class stratified societies.[79]

A more comprehensive picture of social structures in rural Africa is obtained when Kitching's analysis is read together with that of Stavenhagen which was reviewed on pages 79—80 above.

Class Struggle

One of the important consequences of colonialism in tropical Africa was that it shifted the focus of what might be called the principal contradiction, which was hitherto between the ruling classes and the masses of the ruled, especially in those areas in which more sophisticated political organizations (states and empires) had emerged: In the face of foreign capitalist penetration and domination, internal class antagonisms were temporarily set aside when the main contradiction now came to be viewed as the one between the colonized and the colonizers. And to the extent that the process of colonization was facilitated or mediated by groups of local collaborators, it has been shown quite frequently that such ready collaboration was not only based on local class interests, but was even more forthcoming in those particular areas in which communal relations were or had already broken up to a very significant degree. Walter Rodney states, for example, that

> Although class divisions were not pronounced in African society, they too contributed to the ease with which Europe imposed itself commercially on large parts of the African continent. The rulers had a certain status and authority, and when bamboozled by European goods they began to use that position to raid outside their own societies as well as to exploit internally by victimizing some of their own subjects. In the simplest of societies where there were no kings, it proved impossible for Europeans to strike up the alliance which was necessary to carry on a trade in captives on the coast. *In those societies with ruling groups, the association with Europeans was easily established; and afterwards Europe had hardened the existing internal class divisions and created new ones.*[80] (My emphasis.)

Since we have reaffirmed the view that the Western or classical model of class formation was not reproduced (at least not in its exact form) in tropical Africa, we are faced with the problem of terminology at the outset of an analysis of the concept of class struggle. Have such labels as "bourgeoisie", "petty bourgeoisie", "proletariat", and so forth, which Marx used to categorize the different interest groups in his studies of Western societies any useful purpose in the African context? The first thing to remember, of course, is that it is not the *labels in themselves* that are important, but the *reality* which they describe and enable us to perceive and comprehend as a *material fact*.

Although some writers on African society, such as Samir Amin, have asserted that a national bourgeoisie had emerged in some parts of tropical Africa, e.g., in the British colonies of West Africa, it is generally accepted that no national bourgeoisie of any significance developed in tropical Africa, and that therefore, it would be inappropriate to apply this term to the African ruling classes.[81]

The principal contradiction within colonial society was and is being "resolved" through nationalist struggles which are essentially *class* struggles even though they take different forms according to local conditions. Which label or name shall we attach to the nationalists who lead these struggles against colonialism, and who subsequently become the new ruling elements at independence?

Some writers, such as Amilcar Cabral, have termed this stratum, which led the nationalist movements, "petty bourgeoisie", and contrasted its position with that of its counterparts in Western Europe. This led Cabral to the conclusion that while the petty bourgeoisie in the West must be regarded as a class which serves but "does not determine the historical orientation of the country", the African petty bourgeoisie is endowed with the function of ruling, i.e., they become a *ruling class* at independence. And in reference to the question of class antagonism, Cabral declares that

The moment national liberation comes and the petty bourgeoisie takes power, we enter, or rather return to history, and thus the internal contradictions break out again.[82]

The application of the term petty bourgeoisie to the African situation can, therefore, be justified on several grounds: the African ruling classes are not a national bourgeoisie because, unlike their counterpart in the West, they did not emerge from a mature or decaying feudal system; they lack the economic base as merchants, bankers, capitalist entrepreneurs on which the bourgeoisie in the West was firmly enchored; and finally, the African ruling class is only a *junior partner* in its economic relationship with the international bourgeoisie, of which it is an *integral part*.

The concept of class struggle is inseparable from *political struggle*, and its main objective is to alter the existing, exploitative class relations: this is an important point because it means, in fact, that class struggle is directed against those who wield the instruments of *state power*.[83] This viewpoint, furthermore, points to the belief in Marxist class analysis that class struggle is the motive force for change, and that it is the social system itself which is the source or generator of social, economic, cultural and political problems. This view is diametrically opposed to that held by the social stratification-social élite theorists as typified by writers such as Lloyd who belives that

Social change results from continual interaction between individuals and groups seeking, through their use of existing resources and new opportunities, to improve their position in the social hierarchy.[84]

Seen in this way, social change results from the efforts of persons acting individually or in small groups and in competition against others according to agreed norms (as previously pointed out) for positions of power, prestige or occupational status *within a given* social system: significantly, according to this view, the social system itself is not *questioned or challenged*.

Lloyd affirms that structural change results from the actions of individuals, and even more importantly, that where the states of tropical Africa are concerned, changes which have and are occurring within them, have nothing or little to do with their own internal contradictions but stem from external sources:

...On occasion external factors, not specifically the product of any process internal to the society, provides totally new situations—such of course is the impact of Western industrial nations on the tropical world. The individual continually seizes these new opportunities thus presented to him, exploits them in his own interest, and in so doing possibly changes the structure of his own society, inasmuch as he redefines some norms of behaviour or creates a new status.[85]

Although this passage is couched in cautious terms, it is nonetheless intended as a serious challenge to the concept of social change as formulated in terms of class contradictions and class struggle. From here Lloyd proceeds to challenge the theory of class more directly, when, with one stroke of the pen, he dismisses Marx as an "evolutionary thinker" whose approach to the development of societies through successive stages was too *deterministic*.

Lloyd argues that Marx's theory of class struggle is unacceptable because it postulates the inevitability of the intensification of the class struggle, leading, inevitably, to revolution in which the lower classes will eventually, and inevitably overthrow the upper classes. This obvious distortion of Marx's theory of class struggle and revolution enables the protagonists of the élite theory to "prove", as Lloyd claims here, that Marx has been *wrong* in his predictions because "the intensification of class struggle leading to revolution does not always occur (and has occurred where Marx least expected it").[86]

Showing an appalling ignorance of Marx's theory of class and class struggle, Lloyd proceeds to suggest a reformulation of this theory in order to make it "relevant" and acceptable to the conservatives. He claims that when reformulated, the Marxist thesis would result in correcting the "bias of sociological theories which attempt to study change as a process internal to the institutional structure of society".[87]

Such a reformulation, according to Lloyd, would then stress that even when class struggle is intensified, change in social relations would still be seen to be dependent on the degree to which privileged groups themselves are able to cope with the threat from below because

The measures taken by these various groups may result in the actualization of the new relationships leading to a change in the institutions of society; but conversely they may be compensatory, leaving the institutions intact—though not removing the source of the contradiction. As thus expressed, change is not inevitable.[88]

Although we entirely agree with Lloyd that the ruling classes, whenever threatened by the oppressed, will take the necessary steps to *contain, eliminate* or *redirect* such challenges and prospective social changes, which, otherwise would mean their ruin. However, we dispute Lloyd's relegation of the masses to the position of mere spectator on the political scene as he has claimed previously. We shall say more about this shortly, when Lloyd's misconceptions and distortions of the Marxian theory of class and class struggle will be further exposed.

CLASS CONSCIOUSNESS

The concept of class consciousness plays a very important role in the Marxist theory of class, of which it is an integral part. At the stage when societies break up into antagonistic strata on the basis of *class interests*, the degree of "class" consciousness is very low in the exploited social strata. Under these conditions, therefore, the nature of class struggle that may occur must be expected to be more latent than manifest or "pure". At any rate, as we have already indicated, class struggle takes different forms depending on the concrete historical conditions and circumstances.

The following passage by Marx should help to clear the distortions and misconceptions which are prevalent in the concepts of class struggle and the development of class consciousness. He writes:

Just as the *economists* are the scientific representatives of the bourgeois class, so the *Socialists* and the *Communists* are the theoreticians of the proletarian class. So long as the proletariat is not yet sufficiently developed to constitute itself as a class, and consequently so long as the struggle itself of the proletariat with the bourgeoisie has not yet assumed a political character, and the productive forces are not yet sufficiently developed in the bossom of the bourgeoisie itself to enable us to catch a glimpse of the material conditions necessary for the emancipation of the proletariat and for the formation of a new society, these theoreticians are merely utopians who, to meet the wants of the oppressed classes, improvise systems and go in search for a regenerating science.[89] (Emphasis in the original.)

It is most important to stress the fact that Marx, Lenin, Mao Tse-tung and other great socialist leaders have placed great emphasis on the *actual processes* by which the development of class and political consciousness of the oppressed classes take place. In other words, all these revolutionary leaders have never subscribed to the notion that the existence of exploitation and oppression and/ or the awareness on the part of the dominated classes of their *objective class position*, would lead, automatically, to the development of class consciousness and revolution.[90]

In his contribution to the further clarification of the concept of the proletariat and its supposed historical task, Lukács has argued, for example, that

... It would be a mechanistic application of Marxism, and therefore a totally unhistorical illusion, to conclude that a correct proletarian class consciousness—adequate to the proletariat's leading role—can gradually develop on its own, without both frictions and setbacks, *as though the proletariat could gradually evolve ideologically into a revolutionary vocation appropriate to its class.*[91] (My emphasis.)

Among some of the most decisive factors in the development of class consciousness of the oppressed working classes are *organization* and *mobilization*. A revolutionary movement and leadership, armed with a revolutionary ideology, is essential to provide a theoretical and practical orientation to the masses. Because the masses can only *learn meaningfully through action and practical demonstration*, it is through direct involvement in historical struggles at various levels that workers, peasants and the rest of the oppressed masses will develop and deepen their class consciousness. More will be said about mobilization later.

Mao Tse-tung has stressed the role played by organization in the development and formation of man's correct thoughts. He shows that at the stage when the proletariat engages in spontaneous struggles, e.g., machine-smashing in factories, it is a "class-in-itself",

But when it reaches the second stage of its practice, the period of conscious and organized economic and political struggles, the proletariat was able to comprehend the essence of capitalist society, the relations of exploitation between social classes and its own historical task; ... It was then that the proletariat became a "class-for-itself".[92]

By presenting a distorted version of the Marxian theory of class consciousness, i.e., without taking into consideration the actual conditions for its emergence and development, writers like Lloyd, make it easy for themselves to claim, first, that Marx's theory is too deterministic, and secondly, on the basis of the most superficial observation, to claim and conclude that class consciousness is absent among the African masses and that therefore African societies are devoid of social classes. Lloyd pursues these claims and allegations, for example, in a paper in which he examines the subject of class consciousness among the Yoruba of Western Nigeria.[93]

Although in this paper, Lloyd purports to be merely presenting to his readers the views of the Yoruba élites on the subject, it only takes a cursory look to discover that its contents and conclusions are those of Lloyd himself. In other words, Lloyd appears to be using the views of the Yoruba élites merely to affirm his own firmly held views—the views and opinions selected are those which seem to "fit" well into a preconceived analytical frame.[94]

However, the paper fails, as one would have expected, to demonstrate the "absence" of class consciousness among the masses. Instead, Lloyd only succeeds in pointing out that there are mitigating factors which seriously impede or militate against the development of such class consciousness in the African workers, peasants and the rest of the masses. But this is what Marx, Lenin, Mao and others have stressed on the basis of both their *theoretical* and *practical* involvement in the organizing and mobilizing of the masses for political struggles. The existence of mitigating factors, which must be viewed most seriously at every stage in any political struggle, does not and cannot, however, by itself constitutes proof that class consciousness is either absent or will not emerge and develop under the appropriate conditions.[95]

On the question of dogmatism, we would like to point out that no *serious* Marxist would regard Marxism as a dogma, but rather as a guide to scientific investigation and practice. The ongoing debates and mutual criticisms among some Marxists is proof of this. It is important to point out furthermore in this respect, that many of these serious debates centre around the very serious questions of "dogmatism" and "determinism". And in some of these debates, the notion "of the historical tasks" of the proletariat have been examined and re-examined in the light of both past and recent historical experiences in class struggles. As a result of these critical exchanges among Marxist theorists, important concessions of error or mistaken ideas, have been made from time to time. Thus, for instance, writing in 1970, Paul M. Sweezy asserted that

In classical Marxian theory ... the concept of the proletariat, was, of course, quite clear and specific: it referred to the wage workers employed in large-scale capitalist industry who, in the advanced capitalist countries, constituted a majority of the working class and a very substantial proportion of the total population. These workers were assumed to have acquired, as a consequence of the capitalist accumulation process itself, certain specifically proletarian (and anti-bourgeois) attitudes and values: solidarity, cooperativeness, egalitarianism, etc. Historically speaking, the proletarian was seen as a 'new man' formed by capitalism and possessing the interest, the will, and the ability to overthrow the system and to lead the way in the construction of a new socialist society.[96]

Sweezy was later challenged by Charles Bettelheim, and in his reply he admitted:

I wrote this not after research in the relevant texts but from my general understanding of Marxian theory formed after a period of many years. Subsequently I was challenged to support this intepretation, and I must confess that I was unable to do so. It is easy to cite dozens of passages from the works of Marx and Engels affirming the rovelutionary role of the proletariat in the overthrow of capitalism. I have not, however, found any which are specifically addressed to the question of the proletariat's ability or readiness to build a socialist society; and at least some of their formulations, especially those which analyse the effects of the division of labour on the worker, clearly imply a negative evaluation of the proletariat's qualifications.[97]

Some of the "negative evaluations" which Sweezy still seems to sense only somewhat vaguely, have been elaborated and expressed, quite unequivocally by Lenin who, according to Lukács, declared that ". . . the path to ultimate victory of the proletariat is long and passes through many defeats, and not only material setbacks but also ideological regressions are unavoidable on the way".[98] And both because and as a result of this, Lukács adds, ". . . there will always be proletariat strata who will *stand passively by* and watch the liberation struggle of their own class, and *even cross over to the other side*—the more so, the more developed the capitalism".[99] (My emphasis.)

Lloyd knows some of the main causes of these setbacks very well, and is even aware that they are being artificially and consciously generated by the ruling classes in their attempt to avert revolutions or revolutionary changes. Commenting on conditions in the course of class struggle in which the ruling classes make attempts to defend and preserve their positions of power and privilege from the oppressed classes, Lloyd states that

Such situations could in most cases be termed one of class conflict. Yet in the poorer nations—and espicially those of Africa and Asia, but less so in Latin America—the concept of class is alien to most of the population. *Ideologies of national unity and consensus are successfully promoted and conflicts are frequently expressed in ethnic terms. Yet, as I hope to illustrate, these merely disguise conflicts of interest expressed in terms of power and wealth.*[100] (My emphasis.)

However, the promise that Lloyd makes, namely to show us how the ruling classes go about effecting this disguise of *conflict of interest*, fails to materialize. Instead, Lloyd proceeds to *join hands* with the ruling classes in the *promotion* of these same ideologies—he becomes one of their *intellectual articulators*. In his assiduous efforts to promote the ideologies of tribalism, classlessness, African socialism,[101] and so forth, Lloyd not only allies himself with the African ruling classes, but he also reveals his own political and philosophical world outlook. His

94

motives against the use of class analysis in Africa are revealed more clearly, when, for example, he compares the two main methods of sociological investigation, namely the functional/integration model and the conflict model.

In rejecting the conflict model and embracing the functional method, Lloyd tries to show at the same time that, as a matter of fact, he is not alone in this since the conflict model is generally rejected in Western Europe, where, according to him, most social scientists have a strong feeling of repugnance against Marxism. The African élites too, Lloyd affirms, not only view Marxism as a *foreign* or *alien* ideology, but they too show this strong repugnance and revulsion to Marxism.[102]

And when Lloyd registers his final rejection to the use of class analysis in African studies, it then becomes abundantly clear that he does so not because he really believes that there is no class system in African societies, or that the oppressed have no class consciousness and therefore there is no class struggle: Lloyd *rejects* class analysis (*Marxism*) because, as he puts it himself,

> To describe the process of social change in terms of class conflict suggests an acceptance of a Marxist analysis.[103]

TRIBALISM

In the *context* of colonialism and neo-colonialism, tribalism is the product of these very processes. The colonial administrators used "tribalism" as an instrument whereby, for example, the authority of traditional rulers (as collaborators) was sustained in order to ensure more effective colonial control.[104]

In his eagerness to promote the tribal consciousness, Lloyd does not even pause to consider the possibility that tribalism and class might, in certain cases, be compatible rather than mutually exclusive phenomena as he seems to assume. Lloyd also fails to take into account the important fact that there might not only be *one but two or more types* of tribal or ethnic consciousness. In drawing attention to this important distinction, Archie Mafeje, for example, also demonstrated the true nature of tribal consciousness:

> This is not to deny the existence of tribal ideology and sentiment in Africa. The argument is that they have to be understood—and conceptualized—differently under modern conditions. There is a real difference between the man who, on behalf of his tribe, strives to maintain its traditional integrity and autonomy, and the man who invokes tribal ideology in order to maintain a power position, not in the tribal area, but in the modern capital city, and whose ultimate aim is to undermine and exploit the supposed tribesmen. The fact that it works, as is often pointed out by tribal ideologists, is no proof that 'tribes' or 'tribalism' exist in any objective sense. If anything, it is a mark of *false consciousness* on the supposed tribesmen, who subscribe to an ideology that is inconsistent with their material base and therefore unwittingly respond to the call for their own exploitation. On the part of the new African élite, it is a ploy or distortion they use to conceal their exploitative role. It is an ideology in the original Marxist sense and they share it with their European fellow-ideologists.[105] (Emphasis in the original.)

It is in an attempt to conceal or de-emphasize class divisions and exploitation that pedlars in tribalism stress ethnic loyalties or the unbroken tribal ties between the élite and village brethren. Thus when Lloyd, for instance, suggests that the African élites are still recruited from a "humble social background", or that despite their educational achievements the élites still maintain links with their village, the aim is to "prove" that channels to élite positions and status remain open, ensuring so-called social mobility. And even more important, the conclusion we are expected and supposed to draw from all this is that social relations between the élites and the masses do not involve exploitation, since in maintaining links with their village, the élites continue to give financial support to their family and kin, ensuring thereby a redistribution of wealth through the extended family system.[106]

Because his own analysis, for example, of income distribution in Asia, Africa and Latin America convinces him that conditions of ruthless exploitation do in fact exist, Lloyd feels compelled to offer some criticism against the exploiters. Such criticism, however, is nothing more than a *liberal, moral reproach* against the ruling classes: Lloyd implies that there is nothing seriously wrong with the social system as such, although he admits that it is not "perfect"; there is *absolutely* nothing wrong with *élitism*, but what is wrong is that some of the élites are greedy, selfish, and lack self-discipline and modesty.

Where colonialism and neo-colonialism are concerned, Lloyd is able to show, though in a superficial manner, that the relationship between the metropoles and their former colonies was and continues to be based on the exploitation of one by the other. (See footnote 109 below.) But in his determination to minimize and de-emphasize the nature and degree of this exploitation and subsequent conflict in this relationship, Lloyd drives himself into a position where he ends up an apologist of both colonialism and neo-colonialism.

For example, against the assertion that the main preoccupation of colonial administrations was the maintenance of "law" and "order", rather than the provision of social welfare and social services to the colonized, Lloyd, who makes a comparison between the British and French administrations, claims and implies that this preoccupation was not motivated by the need to exploit and make profit, but it was simply that "common to both . . . was an extreme pausity of officials and the consequent emphasis simply on the maintenance of law and order rather than on policies directed towards creating rapid economic development which might produce social dislocation".[107]

And while Lloyd concedes that well established Nigerian businessmen and traders were forced out of business by colonial trading companies, he is quick to add and stress that "Nevertheless . . . expatriate companies did provide training for a large number of agents, some of whom subsequently started operations on their own."[108]

Although it is admitted that under conditions of neo-colonialism, the so-called partnership, for instance, in the area of foreign aid to the underdeveloped nations, involves exploitation of the recipient by the donor, yet this partnership, according to Lloyd, must be maintained:

When partnership with the industrial nations seemingly yields decreasing rewards, the outright seizure of their assets to control the distribution of profits seems the most attractive course. *Yet one must not kill the goose that lays the golden eggs. To ruin an industry which dominates the national economy would mean increased unemployment and poverty.*[109] (My emphasis.)

In this respect, it is claimed once again, that although the oppressed are bound to become aware of the fact that they are being exploited, this awareness will never rise from ethnic to class consciousness:

Inevitably people of the more backward areas begin to feel that they are being exploited by those of the richer areas and because poverty is identified with territory rather than with social class the contest is seen as lying between ethnic groups.[110]

In support of this pontification, Lloyd quotes with implicit approval but without comment, one of the champions of the notion of "equal opportunity", the former British Prime Minister, Edward Heath, who solemnly declared at the United Nations General Assembly in 1970 that

Moreover, we must recognize a new threat to the peace of the nations, indeed to the very fabric of society. We have seen in the last few years the growth of a cult of political violence, preached and practised not so much between states as within them. It is a sombre thought but it may be that in the 1970s civil war, not war between nations, will be the main danger we will face.[111]

We must not allow ourselves to be hoodwinked or taken in by statements such as this one. Their purpose is to distort the true nature of the relationship between capitalist countries and underdeveloped nations in order to conceal, among other things, the close collaboration that exists among ruling classes across national or state boundaries, and especially that between Britain and her former colonies of tropical Africa which are the focus of Lloyd's analysis. Generally speaking, we know, for example, that a large proportion of the foreign aid bill is set aside by the capitalist countries for training and building up of police forces in the underdeveloped countries of Asia, Africa and Latin America, and that these police forces are used for the suppression of internal organizations which seek a radical and meaningful changes of the structure of their societies. This aid, like the outright military aid given by the same countries, is therefore, intended as support for reactionary regimes in the underdeveloped countries.

This question has been examined by Keith Buchanan, among others, who has recently provided irrefutable data to demonstrate the extent and degree to which the capitalist countries are involved in maintaining "law and order" in support of their *class allies* in the underdeveloped countries. He demolishes the claims contained in the statement quoted above in the following way:

97

... In this great belt of slums the most distinctive type of conflict is less that *between* states than that *within* states, resuling from increasing determination of the damned and disinherited to overturn the dominating clique of self-serving, externally-oriented politicians and refashion society along new and more human lines. And so the Third World is 'gray' in another sense, too, for the distinction between unrest, civil disobedience and civil war is nowhere clear cut and the distinction between police and military, both preoccupied with 'Containing' change, is at the best arbitrary distinction.[112] (Emphasis in the original.)

In the table below, Buchanan shows the amount of "police aid" given by the United States to a few countries as an example of that country's commitment to the support of the ruling classes of those countries:

Table 2. *US police assistance 1961—9 per head of 1970 population ($)*

Asia		Africa		Latin America	
Thailand	2.01	Liberia	2.45	Guyana	1.27
Laos	1.27	Somalia	1.60	Panama	1.07
Jordan	1.12	Ruanda	.32	Dominican R.	.77
Cambodia	.39	Congo Kinshasa	.28	Costa Rica	.75
South Korea	.22	Ethiopia	.12	Salvador	.56

Source: K. Buchanan, *The Geography of Empire* (Spokesman Books, 1972) p. 15.

MOBILIZATION

By way of rounding up our analysis of class struggle and class consciousness, we wish to say a few words about the concept of mobilization. This brief discussion is intended to clarify further the notions of class struggle and class consciousness by linking them to some concrete historical experience of our time. By so doing we hope to show, first, the dynamic nature of the concept of mobilization, the dynamism which is almost completely obscured in the treatment of the concept by exponents of theories of élites, of modernization and of community development. Secondly, we intend to falsify some of the conservative claims that African workers, peasants and the masses at large have no *potential and ability* to sustain a revolutionary struggle.[113]

While the protracted armed struggles in Southern Africa that have been raging over the past ten years and more is an internationally recognized historical fact, we have the extraordinary situation in which some Western social scientists, while boasting that they have been doing research on Africa for the past twenty years and more, yet don't seem to have become aware of these national liberation struggles.[114]

Lloyd, who has written most of his books on Africa (todate) between 1966 and 1974, the same period during which the nationalist movements in the former Portuguese colonies of Mozambique, Angola and Guinea-Bissau rose and successfully challenged one of the most intransigent colonial powers, makes no reference whatsoever in all his writings about these *peasant* revolutions. The explanation is not difficult to find: quite obviously these successful peasant revolutionary struggles *do not fit* into his *pre-conceived* analytical frame of reference. The long-drawn revolutionary struggles of these former colonial territories in Africa which have ended in defeat against Portuguese colonialism falsify and demolish Lloyd's strongly held assumptions about the lack of revolutionary potential and class consciousness in the peasantry in general, and in the African peasantry in particular.[115] Failure even to mention these events in passing amounts to an attempted distortion, by omission, of social reality and an intellectual dishonesty.

The historical experiences of the struggles for national liberation in the former Portuguese colonies greatly illuminate our discussion of class struggle and the development of political and class consciousness because it is in these territories, particularly in Mozambique and Guinea-Bissau, where the liberation movements have evolved the most revolutionary parties and leadership.[116]

The Swedish political scientist, Lars Rudebeck, has recently undertaken a field study of Political Mobilization in Guinea-Bissau, under the dynamic leadership of the PAIGC. Rudebeck examines the whole liberation struggle carried out by the people of this tiny Africa country, but we are only interested for our purpose here, in his analysis of the concept of mobilization in the context of a concrete historical situation.[117]

To Rudebeck, "... mobilization in a broader sense, or social mobilization, is more or less equivalent to the *growth of social and political consciousness*".[118] (My emphasis.) Rudebeck sees mobilization as comprised of two separate but related aspects, and these, in his own excellent summary, are as follows:

I. *Social Mobilization*
1. Ever on-going process whereby people's awareness of the structural conditions and contradictions of society is influenced by these conditions and contradictions themselves. This process may be intensified, thus leading to sharpened awareness
    (a) spontaneously, as a result of objective conditions
    (b) as a result of political mobilization
    (c) through a combination of the two.

II. *Political Mobilization*
1. Process involving the political organization and participation of the people
    (a) spontaneously, arising from the 'grass-roots'.
    (b) as a result of organizational, ideological, and socio-economic work initiated by conscious minorities for purposes of increased social mobilization
    (c) through a combination of the two.[119]

Seen in this light, and thus defined, the concept of mobilization is very much in accord with the way in which we understand the concepts of class struggle and class consciousness and their development. It is this correct conceptualization of the concept which enables Rudebeck to see it further in its *dynamic* context as "... the crucial political process and mechanism through which political leaders organize support for revolutionary efforts by appealing to the people's experienced and concrete interests in a better life".[120]

This way of conceptualizing the notion of mobilization contrasts most sharply with the *abstract way* in which mobilization has been treated by protagonists of the theories of modernization, development and of community development.[121]

Under a revolutionary party and leadership, the process of mobilization becomes a powerful instrument through which political and class consciousness, i.e., a revolutionary *potential* can be nurtured, developed and transformed into necessary strength for the execution of a class struggle. And to mobilize effectively requires a knowledge and understanding of both the internal and external socio-economic system against which the class struggle is directed; but in turn this knowledge and understanding become sharpened and deepened by the mobilization process and experience.

The central questions and issues confronting the particular liberation struggle, the aims and objectives of that struggle, the relationships of the various social strata involved in the struggle—all these and many other questions are defined, redefined and clarified during the course of the struggle.[122]

The most cursory examination of successful revolutionary armed struggles will show that their victory, often against an enemy many times stronger than the nationalist movement itself, was due, among the most important and decisive factors, to a *conscious, political, ideological* and *organizational mobilization*, rather than to some supposed and mythical role or "historical task" of this or that stratum of a given society, a role imputed to the particular group without insisting on the existence of the appropriate conditions.[123]

Summary and Conclusions

This paper has set out to critically analyse some of the conventional models of social analysis that have been increasingly exported from the Western capitalist countries since after the Second World War to tropical Africa and other parts formely colonized by these imperialist countries. Our analysis has focused specially on the theories of modernization, dualism, community development and the notion of élite—the latter in conjunction with the Marxist theory of class and class struggle. The inherent weaknesses and the political and ideological objectives and uses of these theories have been exposed.

And finding them to be theoritically inadequate; to lack universal validity and to be ineffective policy-wise, we have, as others have already done, called for the rejection of these theories and export models of development. We have called for their rejection because, even more important, these theories contribute to the intensification and deepening of the socio-economic and developmental problems of the underdeveloped countries rather than help find effective remedies for their liquidation.

In our analysis of the theory of class and class struggle, we have shown how the protagonists of the theories of social stratification and social élites in the African context, have systematically attempted to distort and modify both the notion of élite as seen and conceptualized by its classical formulators, and the Marxist theory of class and class struggle, before offering the former as the appropriate and only relevant model for the analysis and study of Africa.

After a detailed examination of the main claims, assumptions and some of the main objections to the use of class analysis advanced by the protagonists of the theories of élites, we came to the conclusion that, on the contrary, class analysis is not only relevant but the only appropriate theory and method for the study of the socio-economic problems of the independent states of tropical Africa and other parts of the underdeveloped countries experiencing imperialist domination and exploitation. In conclusion, we would like to stress the grounds on which our rejection of the theory of élite is based, namely that:

1. the theory of élite is a conservative theory which sees rule by a minority over a supposedly passive majority and its concomitant aspects of domination, exploitation and oppression, as natural and inevitable. It is a miserable theory of *political inertia* which seeks to justify and maintain the status quo. The theory of élite in both its classical and contemporary formulation, fails to explain the forces of social, economic, political and cultural change.

2. the theory of élite does not enable us to grasp fully the causes of social problems and the factors which generate the necessary changes in the social relations of production, exchange and distribution because it erroneously posits and locates these problems in the individual or in small groups, rather than in the social system which it regards as *given and sacrosanct*.

3. in the face of all the evidence provided throughout this entire paper, the theory of élites must be rejected and be superseded by the theory of class and class struggle in the study of Africa. It is only through the use of class analysis that we come to perceive how class societies, in Africa and elsewhere, evolve and develop through the ages. The theory of class and class struggle, which is diametrically opposed to the theory of élites, rejects the assertion that domination, exploitation, social inequality and poverty, are natural and inevitable, and it offers guidance or guide lines to the oppressed as to how they can proceed to *collectively organize* in order to effectively challenge and *liberate themselves* from the system that oppresses them. If this paper succeeds in stimulating more interest and in persuading scholars on Africa to reject the received wisdom in research methods it will have made a worthwile contribution to the study of Africa.

NOTES

1. Meisel, James, H., *The Myth of the Ruling Class: Gaetano Mosca and the "Élites".* (Ann Arbor, Chicago University Press, 1958) p. 366.
Nadel, S. F., "The Concept of Social Élites". *International Social Science Bulletin (UNESCO), Vol. VIII, No. 1,* 1956, pp. 413—424.

Mitchell, J. C., and Epstein, A. L., "Occupational Prestige and Status among Urban Africans in Northern Rhodesia", in *Africa: Social Problems of Change and Conflict*, edited by Pierre van den Berghe (Chandler Publishing Company, San Francisco, 1965) p. 198.

2. Cohen, Robin, "Class in Africa: Analytical Problems and Perspectives", in *The Socialist Register*, edited by Ralph Miliband and J. Saville (The Merlin Press, London, 1972) p. 252.

3. Meisel, J. H., op.cit., p. 14.

Meisel pays tribute to the work of Robert Michels, showing that the latter, who had an advantage over Mosca as he had studied some of the modern mass organizations in Germany, could have most certainly had advanced Mosca's own works had he not been unduly influenced by Mosca (op.cit., page 184). On page 189, Meisel makes the following comments:

> Robert Michels almost recognized the paramount significance of the organizational phenomenon, but since he *concentrated his attention on the 'governing minorities', the other aspect of organization, its mass character remained blurred in his important study.* And that, too, may be attributed to Mosca's influence: to the old teacher's tendency to put organized minorities in opposition to the unorganized majority. *The possibility that millions of men might be organized and be articulate, that they might be informed enough to exchange places with their leaders—such possibilities would have been utterly denied by our two authors. Mosca saw his 'balance of the social forces' upset by the new, 'plebian' parties; Michels reassured him that they could not possibly succeed.* The very notion that they could one day become the focus, the decisive factor in determining the character and range of the new social and political élites would have been incomprehensible to Gaetano Mosca and his alter ego. (My emphasis.)

Bottomore, T. B., *Élites and Society* (Penguin Books, 1964) p. 15.

4. Meisel, J. H., op.cit., passim.

5. Ibid., op.cit., pp. vi and 8.

Mannheim, Karl, *Ideology and Utopia: An Introduction to the Sociology of Knowledge*, (Routledge and Kegan Paul, 1936). On page 139, Mannheim has written:

> One of the most impressive facts about modern life is that in it, unlike preceding cultures, intellectual activity is not carried on exclusively by a *socially rigidly defined class*, such as a priesthood, *but rather by a social stratum which is to a large degree unattached to any social class and which is recruited from an increasingly inclusive area of social life.* This sociological fact determines essentially the uniqueness of the modern mind, which is characteristically not based upon the authority of a priesthood, which is not closed and finished, but which is rather dynamic, elastic, in a constant state of flux, and perpetually confronted by new problems. Even humanism was already largely the expression of such a more or less *socially emancipated stratum*, and where the nobility became the bearer of culture it broke through the fixedness of a classbound mentality in many respects. But not until we come to the period of bourgeois ascendency does the *level of cultural life become increasingly detached from a given class.* (My emphasis.)

Mills, C. Wright, *The Power Élite*, (Oxford University Press, 1956).

Bottomore, T. B., op.cit., see pages 24—44.

Sweezy, P. M., "Power Élite or Ruling Class?", in *Monthly Review*, September 1956. This is a review article of Mills' book.

Poulantzas, Nicos, *Political Power and Social Classes*, (New Left Books and Sheed and Ward, 1973) pp. 99—119, and see especially pages 325—330 for analysis of the theory of élites.

Various attempts have been made by later élite theorists, such as Mills, to integrate certain elements of the theory of élites into the general Marxist theory, but these attempts have generally failed. Part of this failure was due to the fact that often these theorists have wrongly assumed that the theories of Ruling Élite, "Power Élite", and social stratification, were in fact *variants of class analysis*. These attempts have been seriously questioned and exposed at various levels. Consider, for example, the following summary conclusions by Poulantzas:

> The major defect of these theories consists in the fact that they do not provide an *explanation* of the foundation of political power. In addition, they acknowledge a plurality of sources for political power but can offer no explanation for their relations. They thus end in conclusions diametrically opposed to those which they originally envisaged: whilst giving a critique of the distorted Marxist conception of the dominant class, and whilst hoping in particular to examine the functioning peculiar to the bureaucracy, they end up by acknowledging the unity of the political élites. But in their case, this unity remains ideological. As far as the bureaucracy is concerned, since they recognize its own political power, they end up either by reducing its functioning to membership of an imaginary economic group (Mills) or by considering it as the exclusive 'subject' of political power in a narrow sense (the Weberian school) or in a broad sense (Burnham); op.cit., p 330. (Emphasis in the original.)

Wright Mills (op.cit., page 13) defines élites in the following way:

> The élite who occupy the command posts may be seen as the possessors of power and wealth and celebrity; they may be seen as members of the upper stratum of a capitalistic society. They may also be defined in terms of psychological and moral criteria, as certain kinds of selected individuals. So defined, the élite, quite simply, are people of superior character and energy.
>
> ... *They are élite because of the kind of individuals they are.* The rest of the population is *mass*, which, according to this conception, *sluggishly relaxes into uncomfortable mediocrity.* (My emphasis.)

And in a footnote on page 365, Mills adds, *significantly* that

> The conception of the élite as members of a top social stratum, is, of course, in line with the *prevailing common-sense view of stratification.* Technically, *it is closer to 'status group' than to 'class'*, and has been very well stated by Joseph A. Schumpeter, 'Social Classes in an Ethnically Homogenous Environment', etc. (My emphasis.)

6. Bottomore, T. B., op.cit., p. 16.
7. Cited in Meisel, op.cit., p. 351. On the same page, Meisel adds that "The meaning of the term 'free competition' is not clear. If it refers to independent candidates soliciting votes outside or against the well-established parties, then free competition would not be a typical mark of the democratic process as we know it. Schumpeter himself feels some uneasiness about this point: though democratic competition 'excludes many ways of securing leadership which should be excluded, such as competition by military insurrection, it does not exclude the cases which are strikingly analogous to the economic phenomena we label 'unfair' or 'fraudulent' competition or restraint of competition. And we cannot exclude them because if we did we should be left with a completely unrealistic ideal'."

Furthermore, Meisel quotes the *older* Mosca as saying:

> When we say that the voters 'choose' their representative we are using a language that is very inexact. The truth is that the representative *has himself elected* by the voters, and, if that phrase should seem too inflexible and too harsh to fit some cases, we might qualify it by saying that *his friends have him elected.* (Page 106, emphasis in the original.)

Schumpeter, J. A., *Capitalism, Socialism and Democracy*, (London, Allen and Unwin, 1943).

Bottomore, T. B., op.cit. On page 116, Bottomore points out that:

The undemocratic character of representative government becomes most apparent when the representative principle is applied in a system of indirect election, whereby an elected élite itself elects a second élite which is endowed with equal or superior political power. This device has often been resorted to by the opponents of popular rule—a recent example is to be found in the constitution of the Fifth Republic in France under the leadership of de Gaulle—and de Tocqueville, among others, saw in it *an effective means of restricting democracy.* Even when the defenders of the idea of democracy as competition between élites do not propound it *deliberately as a defence against democracy in its other sense —against that incursion of the* masses into politics which de Tocqueville, Pareto, Mosca and Ortega y Gasset unite in deploring—they are still inclined to take representative government as the ideal, *instead of measuring it against the ideal of direct participation by the people in the legislation and administration and looking about for means by which this end might be more closely approached.* (My emphasis.)

8. Ibid., op.cit., pp. 303—304.
   Bottomore, T. B., op.cit., p. 36.
9. Meisel, J. H., op.cit., pp. 113 and 114.
10. Ibid., op.cit., p. 180. On page 11, Meisel shows that the materials with which Mosca and Pareto constructed the theory of the "circulation of élites" came from Marx's doctrine of class struggle, but only with "its proletarian teeth extracted".
11. Ibid., op.cit., pp. 3, 10 and 32. On page 35, Meisel writes that according to Mosca "superior moral fibre will in the long run prevail over superior numbers and brute force; and, secondly, far more important and yet less noted than the first: an *organized minority,* acting in concert, will forever triumph over a *disorganized majority* people without common will or impulse". (My emphasis.) And clarifying further the concept of élite, Meisel writes on page 10:

   This is the antisocialist, specifically anti-Marxist, bent of the élitist theory as it unfolds in the last decade of the nineteenth century. It is the argument by which the middle-class intelligentsia *tries to silence the triumphant propaganda of the revolutionary Left*—as well as its own doubts. *Elitism is a defensive doctrine, a new Dismal Science aimed at the naive optimism of eighteenth-century enlightenment.* The Marxists had inherited that naive confidence, and did not destroy it conclusively in the minds of the bourgeoisie. (My emphasis.)

12. Ibid., op.cit., pp. 117 and 169.
    Bottomore, T. B., op.cit., pp. 17—18.
13. Meisel, J. H., op.cit., p. 119. On page 117, Meisel states: "Mosca rejects the notion of a classless future as an idle dream which is not even beautiful, for awakening from it, if the experiment should be attempted, would be horrible and possibly, 'the end of civilization itself'."
14. Ibid., op.cit., p. 118. On the same page, Meisel raises the pertinent question: "Can the ruling rich be expected to act against their own interest and to make concessions to the poor? The answer would have to be no, if the political class were indeed, as Marx held, nothing more than the 'executive committee' of the wealthy bourgeoisie."
15. Myrdal, Gunnar, *Asian Drama: An Inquiry into the Poverty of Nations, Vol. 1.* (Allen Lane, The Penguin Press, 1968) p. 8.
    Nadel, S. F., op.cit., p. 413.
16. See footnote 15 above.
17. Lloyd, Peter, C., *Africa in Social Change: Changing Traditional Societies in the Modern World* (Penguin Books, Harmandsworth, England, 1967) passim.
18. Lloyd, P. C., *The New Élites of Tropical Africa,* edited, (London, 1966) p. 60. *Classes, Crises and Coups: Themes in the Sociology of Developing Countries,* (Paladin, 1971) p. 101.

19. Lloyd, P. C., *Africa in Social Change* . . ., op.cit., p. 125.
20. Lloyd, P. C., *The New Élites of Tropical Africa*, op.cit., pp. 12—13.
21. Lloyd, P. C., op.cit., (1966) p. 328; (1967) p. 125; (1971) p. 131; *Power and Independence: Urban Africans' Perception of Social Inequality.* (Routledge and Kegan Paul, London, 1974) passim.
22. Lloyd, P. C., op.cit., (1966) p. 13.
23. Ibid., op.cit., p. 51; (1967) p. 126.
24. Lloyd, P. C., op.cit., (1967) p. 240.
    Amin, Samir, *The Class Struggle in Africa, Reprint Number 2.* (Africa Research Group, Cambridge, Mass. 1964) p. 37.
25. Kilson, Martin, "British Colonialism and Transformation of Traditional Élites: Case of Sierra Leone", in *The African Reader: Colonial Africa*, edited by Wilfred Cartey and Martin Kilson (Vintage Books, New York, 1970) pp. 121—122. To stress the significance of the sub-élites, Kilson writes on page 135: "Furthermore, the persons who provided some measure of leadership in peasant risings were often members of the group we have called a subsidiary modern élite: they were semiliterate and, though residing in the rural areas, had more contact than other rural-dwellers with occupations in the cash economy (e.g., as small traders, miners, labourers on cocoa or cotton plantations, catechists in Christian mission, messengers, etc.)."
26. Nadel, S. F., op.cit., p. 417.
27. Lloyd, P. C., op.cit., (1966) p. 50.
28. Kitching, Gavin, N., "The Concept of Class and the Study of Africa", in *The African Review: A Journal of African Politics, Development and International Affairs, Vol. 2, No. 3* (1972) p. 331.
    Nadel, S. F., op.cit., p. 421.
29. Lloyd, P. C., op.cit. (1966) pp. 50—58.
30. Lloyd, P. C., op.cit., (1971) pp. 22 and 144.
31. Ibid., op.cit., p. 130. On the same page, Lloyd writes:
    Political domination must be legitimated, both in the sight of the world at large which expects political leaders to be representative of their people and at home where peace rests upon the acquiescence of the masses.
32. Lloyd, P. C., op.cit., (1966) p. 54; (1967) p. 125: Innovation is understood by Lloyd to mean the readiness and ability to adapt to Western cultural values. See also, op.cit., (1971) p. 129.
33. Nadel, S. F., op.cit., p. 421. Lloyd's ambiguity about whether or not politicians should be regarded as an élite tantamounts to a contradiction: while in one of his definitions he definitely sees the politicians as an élite (see page 73, footnote 21 above), yet in another passage Lloyd seems to make a distinction between *élites* and *politicians.* He states: "The élites are thus beholden to the politicians in power, and dependent on them not only to preserve these privileges, but also to ensure the expansion of the economy so that new offices may be created and promotion prospects enhanced." op.cit., (1967) p. 318. And furthermore, Lloyd has stated that "It is with this relatively small Western aducated élite that the future of West African states largely rests. For this élite now *wields political power.*" op.cit., (1967) p. 125. (My emphasis.)
34. Meisel, J. H., op.cit., pp. 10, 55, and 349.
35. Kitching, G. N., op.cit., p. 330.
36. Lloyd, P. C., op.cit., (1966) p. 60; (1971) p. 101 ff.
37. Lloyd, P. C., op.cit., (1971) p. 101.
38. Lloyd, P. C., op.cit., (1967) pp. 115—119.
39. Lloyd, P. C., op.cit., (1971). On page 20, Lloyd Writes about the Western impact on underdeveloped nations: "I would stress however, first, the nature of new opportunities provided—the growing of cash crops, wage labour in factory and office, positions of power and authority in the new political structure." The ethic of individual or

personal effort and desire to "achieve" receive strong emphasis from Lloyd, op.cit., (1974) pp. 145—147.

40. Lloyd, P. C., op.cit., (1971) pp. 24 and 94.
Hill, Polly, *Studies in Rural Capitalism in West Africa*, (Cambridge, 1970) p. xx.
Halpern, Joel, M., *The Changing Village Community*, (Prentice-Hall, Inc., Engle-wood Cliffs, N. J., 1967) pp. 84—85.
Geertz, Clifford, "A Study of National Character", a review article in *Economic Development and Cultural Change, Vol. 12,* 1962—63. The book under review is Lucien W. Pye's *Politics, Personality, and Nation-Building* (Yale University Press, 1962), in which he makes an assessment of the so-called Westernized élites in Burma. In this review Geertz questions Pye's generalization which, among other things, holds that all Burmese psychological traits are an impediment to "progress" and moderniza-tion. Geertz wonders

> . . . whether, even granting the correctness of his (Pye's) description of Burmese character, some aspects of it may not be facilitative rather than inhibitory of political rationalization and economic growth . . . Even if he is right and the Burmese are hyper-individualistic, distrustful, liable to violence, fond of empty social form, and prefer uncertainty to determinism, is it so clear, especially in the absence of an explicit analysis of Burmese polity and economy as such, that these could not turn out to be very valuable traits in supporting modernization?

41. Lloyd, P. C., op.cit., (1967) p. 92.
42. Lloyd, P. C., op.cit., (1971) p. 92.
43. Lloyd, P. C., op.cit., (1967) p. 110.
44. Stavenhagen, Rodolfo, *Social Classes in Agrarian Societies*, (Anchor Books, 1975).
45. Ibid., op.cit., pp. 76 and 80.
46. Ibid., op.cit., p. 83.
47. Ibid., op.cit., p. 88.
Titmuss, Richard, M., *Commitment to Welfare*, (George Allen and Unwin, 1968).
Townsend, Peter, *The Family Life of Old People*, (Routledge and Kegan Paul, 1957).
Abel-Smith, B., and Townsend, P., *The Poor and the Poorest: Occasional Papers in Social Administration*, (Bell, London, 1965).
All the above authors have written extensively on the problems of inequality, poverty, and the nature and direction of social work as a social service. Insofar as social work is concerned, they represent what might be called the *progressive elements*: they have consistently demanded that social work, *as social service*, must relinguish the practice of focusing on individuals and be redirected to focus on *groups, communities and areas of special need*. In other words, social work must stop being a form of *charity* sponsored by the middle classes (motivated partly by the need to ease their guilty conscience) and become a *liberating* force and process from oppression.
However, we must point out the important fact that as members of the British Labour Movement and the Fabian Society (or at least individuals closely associated with these two movements), they are *committed to welfare*, as Titmuss' book indicates. They are committed to the Welfare State with whose present *imperfections* they are most unhappy. This being the case, the changes they advocate, despite their progressive nature, cannot be expected to bring about radical transformation of society, but they are most likely to make the capitalist system *appear more plausible* to the masses.
48. Fitch, Bob, and Oppenheimer, Mary, *Ghana: End of an Illusion* (Monthly Review Press, 1966) pp. 38—40.
49. Jeffries, Richard, "The Labour Aristocracy? Ghana Case Study", in *Review of African Political Economy, No. 3* (May—October, 1975) pp. 59—70. The quotation is taken from page 62, and the table from page 63.
50. Stavenhagen, R., op.cit., p. 78.
51. Ibid., op.cit., p. 83.

52. Ibid., op.cit., p. 81.
53. Ibid., op.cit., p. 85.
54. Ibid., op.cit., pp. 85 and 87.
55. Lloyd, P. C., op.cit., (1966) p. 61.
56. Kitching, G. N., op.cit., pp. 327—328.
57. Marx, Karl, *Capital, Vol. III*, (Progress Publishers, Moscow, 1959) p. 885.
58. Marx, K., *Surveys From Exile: Political Writings, Vol. 2.*, edited and introduced by David Fernbach. (Penguin Books in association with New Left Books, 1973) p. 239. Frankenberg, Ronald, *Communities in Britain: Social Life in Town and Country.* (Penguin Books, 1966.) On pages 255—6, Frankenberg makes the following important remarks:

> The concept of class has been with us since the Roman census of tax groups, but its present use derives from the nineteenth-century classical political economists and especially from the arguments of Marx and Engels. However, it is not easy to understand what Marx did mean by class for he died before completing Chapter 52 of Volume III of *Capital* in which he was to define the concept. Several people have since completed the fragment of the chapter for him, a task from which Engels wisely abstained, but the most interesting and recent attempt is that made by Ralf Dahrendorf.
> Ralf Dahrendorf ingeniously sets about completing Marx's chapter with a series of quotations from Marx linked together by a commentary. One may object to it, however, by pointing out that the way in which the quotations are arranged makes no allowance for development in Marx's thought. What is clear however is that Marx uses 'class' always in the same general sense, but that he sees it as a concept which changes its meaning in different social situations.

59. Lloyd, P. C., op.cit., (1967) p. 315.
60. Ibid., op.cit., pp. 280 and 308; (1971) pp. 25, 122—123.
61. Lloyd, P. C., op.cit., (1966) p. 60.
62. Kitching, G. N., op.cit., p. 333.
63. Davies, Ioan, *Social Mobility and Political Change*, (McMillan and Company, London, 1970) p. 69.
Cohen, Robin, op.cit., p. 236.
Fanon, Frantz, *The Wretched of the Earth* (Penguin edition, 1961) pp. 119—120. Fanon writes: "The national middle class which takes over power at the end of the colonial regime is an underdeveloped middle class ... (It) is not engaged in production, not invention, not building, nor labour; it is completely canalized into activities of the intermediary type." This passage is quoted in Glyn Hughes in *Socialist Development in Africa, Reprint No. 7* (Africa Research Group, Cambridge, Mass, n.d.) p. 13.
64. Waterman, Peter, "Structure, Contradiction and the Nigerian Catastrophe: Elements of Analysis", (Mimeo, Center of West African Studies, University of Birmingham, June 1970) p. 7.
Cohen, R., op.cit. On page 236, Cohen quotes Martin Kilson to the effect that:

> ... in general, to speak of a middle class implies the existence of two other classes: a lower class and an upper class. In the West African context, the 'lower class' is the mass of African villagers and peasants ... We also include in this category the emergent wagelabouring class, whose general social status is not appreciably better than that of the African peasants. By the 'upper or ruling class' we have in mind the small, but economically and politically dominant, group of European entrepreneurs, business administrators, senior colonial officials, district officers, and the array of lesser colonial servants—what, in short, Sir Ivor Jennings has termed the 'imported oligarchy'.

65. Plotnicov, Leonard, "The Modern African Élite of Jos, Nigeria", in *Social Stratifica-*

tion in Africa, edited by Arthur Tuden and Leonard Plotnicov (The Free Press, N.Y., 1970) p. 299.

66. Lloyd, P. C., *The City of Ibadan: A Symposium on its Structure and Development*, edited by P. C. Lloyd, A. L. Mabogunje, and B. Awe. (Cambridge University Press, 1967) pp. 138 ff.

Allen, V. L., "The Meaning of the Working Class in Africa", in *The Journal of Modern African Studies, 10, 2* (1972) p. 175.

67. Wallerstein, Immanuel, "Class and Class Struggle in Africa", in *Monthly Review, Vol. 26, No. 9* (February, 1975) p. 36.

68. For example:

Amin, Samir, op.cit.;

Rodney, Walter, *How Europe Underdeveloped Africa* (Tanzania Publishing House, Dar es Salaam, 1972:

Davidson, Basil, *The Growth of African Civilization: History of West Africa 1000— 1800* (Longmans, 1965);

Szentes, Tamás, *The Structure of Society and its Changes in the African Countries: Studies on Developing Countries No. 76* (Budapest, 1975). On page 6, Szentes argues that the breaking up of the African communal society was a positive process, but nonetheless, that colonialism had failed in its "historic role". He concludes: "... the export of capitalist society to the colonial territories did not lead to the radical transformation of the indigenous society found there. The colonization evolving in the period and under the circumstances of imperialism (thus particularly the colonization of the interior of Africa) *could not perform even the 'historic function' of transforming and setting in motion the conquered societies.*" (My emphasis.)

69. Rodney, W., op.cit., pp. 235—236.

Amin, Samir, op.cit. On page 25, Amin illustrates the differences in the development of their societies (between Africa and Europe) by pointing out that "The decadence of the village community in the historical conditions of black Africa did not lead either to a society based on slavery or to a feudal society or even less to a capitalist society in the scientific sense of these terms. *That the decadence of the village community did not lead generally in black Africa to a social system corresponding rigorously to one of the two studied by Marx could only surprise a blindfolded dogmatist. Evidently this does not signify that this disintegration did not engender social antagonism.* (My emphasis.)

Stavenhagen, R., op.cit. The author makes the following comments (p. 40): "The analysis of social class structures and stratification has been developed principally in the industrialized capitalist countries. Is this kind of analysis equally applicable to the underdeveloped world? It would seem that the theoretical problems we have already discussed become more complex when the theory is applied to the underdeveloped countries. In the first place, the capitalist system has always served as the classic frame of reference for the structural analysis of social classes. However, *capitalism is never found in a 'pure' state in the Third World* because it has been imported to these countries from the developed world ... Furthermore, because a variety of economic structures and different stages of economic and social evolution coexist in the underdeveloped world, stratifications in these countries have many aspects that they lack in the developed countries. *Consequently, an analysis of social classes in the underdeveloped countries must necessarily proceed differently from one focused on the industrialized societies.*" (My emphasis.)

Marx, K., *Surveys From Exile* ... op.cit. In the introduction on pages 10—11, the following passage, by the editor, brings out some of the differences in stages of development among European countries themselves:

> The starting point of Marx's explanation is the relatively undeveloped character of French capitalism. 'The struggle against capital in its highly developed modern

form—at its crucial point, the struggle of the industrial wage-labourer against the industrial bourgeois—is in France a partial phenomenon.' Industrial capitalism, in other words, was only one of the models of production found concurrently in France, and the great majority of the French population were still involved either in peasant or petty bourgeois (i.e. artisan) production. The lower strata of the middle class had not yet sunk into the proletariat, and in place of the industrial bourgeoisie and proletariat, which the Manifesto presents as the only two classes characteristic of developed industrial capitalism, Marx distinguished a much richer variety of classes and fractions of classes, of which *great land-owners, financial bourgeoisie, industrial bourgeoisie, petty bourgeoisie* (of various gradations), *industrial proletariat, lumpenproletariat,* and *small peasant proprietors* are the only most prominent. (Emphasis in the original); (see footnote 89 on page 111 below).

And similarly, Engels, in reference to class struggle, has stressed the different forms it takes under given historical conditions:

> ... France is the country where, *more than anywhere else, the historical class struggles were each time fought out to a finish,* and where, consequently, the changing political forms within which they move and in which their results are summarised have been stamped in the sharpest outlines. The centre of feudalism in the Middle Ages, the model country, since the Renaissance, of a unified monarchy based on social estates, France demolished feudalism in the Great Revolution and established the rule of the borugeoisie in a *classical purity unequalled by any other European land.* And the struggle of the upward-striving proletariat against the ruling bourgeoisie *appered here in an acute form unknown elsewhere.* (My emphasis.)

This passage is quoted in Lenin, V. I., *Selected Works*, (Progress Publishers, Moscow, 1968) p. 285.

70. Amin, S., op.cit., p. 30.
71. Ibid., op.cit., p. 24.
72. Ibid., op.cit., p. 23.
73. Mao, Tse-tung, *On Practice*, (Peking, 1966) p. 3.
74. Kitching, G. N., op.cit., pp. 348 ff. It is important to keep in mind that what is of greater importance is not the *construction* and provision of *formal models* of class analysis, but the *selection of an appropriate method* of social analysis, and to demonstrate that it is *this particular method* which leads us to the discovery of the concrete facts of social reality rather than another.
75. Ibid., op.cit., p. 348.
76. Kitching, G. N., op.cit., p. 349.
77. Arrighi, Giovanni, "International Corporations, Labour Aristocracies, and Economic Development in Tropical Africa", in *Essays on the Political Economy of Africa*, edited by Giovanni Arrighi and John S. Saul (Monthly Review Press, 1973) pp. 105—151.
78. Jeffries, Richard, op.cit., pp. 59—70.
79. Kitching, G. N., op.cit., p. 340.
80. Rodney, W., op.cit., pp. 55 and 89.
    Although P. C. Lloyd (op.cit., 1971, p. 67) concedes that "the impact of Western industrial nations has destroyed many features of the traditional economy of the poorer nations—by destroying indigenous crafts and trading...", yet he implies that this destruction did not result in the emergence of new social formations along class lines, since, to him, Africa is still a "tribal" and "classless" society.
    Szentes, T., op.cit., p. 17.
81. Rodney, W., op.cit., p. 236.
    Amin, Samir, op.cit., pp. 37—38. On page 38, Amin shows that "Along with these

popular masses in the towns of the former British colonies a real local bourgeoisie has existed for a long time. It is a commercial and financial bourgeoisie of the colonial type, especially at Lagos, whose fortune comes from the big import-export businesses, from the exploitation of the country (usury, etc.), real estate speculation etc. Most of the high officials come from this group which is *strongly allied with the rural bourgeoisie.* On the other hand, in the former French colonies the urban bourgeoisie still *almost entirely composed of non-Africans.* However, the French imperialists have been trying for many years to systematically associate in their enterprises the upper classes of the new bureaucracy, which has thus become the embryo of a real national bourgeoisie of the 'classical' type, which is most often *linked to the traditional chieftains and the rural bourgeoisie of planters."* (My emphasis.)

82. Cabral, Amilcar, *Revolution in Guinea: An African People's Struggle, Stage 1,* (Love and Malcomson, 1969) p. 57.

Lukács, Georg, *History and Class Consciousness: Studies in Marxist Dialectics* (Merlin Press, London, 1968). On page 59, Lukács makes the following comments:

Bourgeoisie and proletariat are the only pure classes in bourgeois society. They are the only classes whose existence and development are entirely dependent on the course taken by the modern evolution of production and only from the vintage point of these classes can a plan for the total organization of society *even be imagined.* The outlook of the other classes (petty bourgeois or peasants) is amambigous or sterile because their existence is not based exclusively on their role in the capitalist system of production but is indissolubly linked with the vestiges of feudal society. (Emphasis in the original.)

83. Schurmann, Franz, *Ideology and Organization in Communist China* (University of California, 1968) p. 518.

84. Lloyd, P. C., op.cit., (1971) p. 18.

85. Ibid., op.cit., p. 73.

86. Ibid., op.cit., p. 77.

87. Ibid., op.cit., p. 77.

88. Ibid., op.cit., p. 77.

Marx, Karl, *The Class Struggle in France 1848—1850,* (Progress Publishers, Moscow, 1972). On page 27, Marx writes:

With the exception of only a few chapters, every more important part of the annals of the revolution from 1848—1849 carries the heading: *Defeat of the revolution!*

What succumbed in these defeats was not the revolution. It was the pre-revolutionary traditional appendages, results of social relationships which had not yet come to the point of sharp class antagonisms—persons, illusions, conceptions, projects from which the revolutionary party before the February Revolution was not free, from which it could be freed not by the *victory of February,* but only by a series of *defeats.*

In a word: the revolution made progress, forged ahead, not by its immediate tragicomic achievements, but on the contrary by the creation of a powerful, united counter-revolution, by the creation of an opponent in combat with whom, only, the party of overthrow ripened into a really revolutionary party. (Emphasis in the original.)

Mészáros, István, "Contingent and Necessary Class Consciousness", in *Aspects of History and Class Consciousness,* edited by I. Mészáros (Routledge and Kegan Paul, London, 1971). On pages 115—116, Mészáros points out:

An objective theory of class consciousness implies above all the assessment of its problematic in terms of the Marxian global conception of capitalism as an actual world system. This means that even the apparently purely local phenomena of social conflict must be related to the objective totality of a given stage of socio-economic development. Without a conscious attempt to link the specific social phenomena to the general trends and characteristics of capitalism as a global system, their significance remains concealed or appears disproportionately magnified, and even the general laws—such as the law of pauperism, the diminishing rate of profit, etc., valid only in globally qualified terms—appear to be nothing but speculations and abstractions. Marx repeatedly stressed that all laws are significantly modified by the manifold specific circumstances interchanging within them in their field of action which embrace—through complex dialectical mediations—the totality of the social system in question. *And, given the prevalence of sufficiently powerful modifying forces, exceptional solutions may very well arise, without affecting in the least the validity of the general laws themselves.* (My emphasis.)

89. Marx, Karl, *The Poverty of Philosophy*, (Progress Publishers, Moscow, 1955) p. 109.
Marx, Karl, *Contribution To The Critique of Political Economy*, (Progress Publishers, Moscow, 1970). On page 21, Marx writes as follows:

> From forms of development of the productive forces these relations turn into their fetters. Then begins an era of social revolution. The changes in the economic foundation lead sooner or later to the transformation of the whole immense superstructure. In studying such transformations it is always necessary to distinguish between the material transformation of the economic conditions of production, which can be determined with the precision of natural science, and the legal, political, religious, artistic or philosophic—in short, ideological forms in which men become conscious of this conflict and fight it out. Just as one does not judge an individual by what he thinks about himself, so one cannot judge such a period of transformation by its consciousness, but, on the contrary, this consciousness must be explained from the contradictions of material life, from the conflict existing between the social forces of production and the relations of production. *No social order is ever destroyed before all the productive forces for which it is sufficient have been developed, and new superior relations of production never replace older ones before the material conditions for their existence have matured within the framework of the old society.* (My emphasis.)

And, in Volume III of *Capital* (op.cit., page 107, footnote 57) Marx has clearly stated that even in the highly developed capitalist systems, class distinctions *do not appear in their pure form*. He comments, on page 885:

> In England, modern society is indispuatably most highly and classically developed in economic structure. Nevertheless, even here the stratification of classes does not appear in its pure form.

90. Lukács, Georg, *Lenin: A Study on the Unity of this Thought*, (New Left Books, 1970) p. 31.
Lenin, V. I., *What Is To Be Done?* (Progress Publishers, Moscow, 1947). This is one of the most important works in which the factors of *organization*, and *social and political mobilization* are discussed and analyzed.

91. Lukács, G., op.cit., (footnote 90 above) p. 24. We would like to stress that we neither believe in, nor subscribe to, *any predestined* "historical mission" assigned to any particular social group, may they be proletariat, peasants or even "élites". We believe that under certain conditions and circumstances, the *potential exists* that a given social group or groups, can, as history has proven, under a revolutionary leadership, act collectively to fundamentally transform thir objective historical conditions and their society.

92. Mao, Tse-tung, op.cit., p. 8.
Mao, Tse-tung, *Selected Readings From the Works of Mao Tse-tung*, (Foreign Languages Press, Peking, 1971). See especially pages 11—40 in which Mao makes a class analysis of Chinese society and also makes an investigation of peasant move-

ments in one area of China.

93. Lloyd, P. C., op.cit., (1966) pp 328—341; (1974) pp. 214—226.
94. Llody, P. C., op.cit., (1974). Lloyd, who boasts that he has been doing research work among the Yorubas of Western Nigeria for the past 25 years, and that his theses have been "proven" consistently, "confesses" that the methods he is using in his investigation are "crude in the extreme", (page 10 and elsewhere). This "confession" has no significance, however, since it is not going to lead to a reappraisal of the author's given model of social analysis (see page 95 above), but merely constitutes a routine practice intended to give protection from criticism by other social scientists.
95. Lloyd, P. C., op.cit., (1966) pp. 331—336.
96. Sweezy, P. M., "The Transition to Socialism", in Monthly Review, Vol. 22, No. 7, (December 1970) p. 17.
   Lenin, V. I., Against Dogmatism and Sectarianism in The Working Class Movement. (Progress Publishers, Moscow, 1965).
   Mao Tse-tung has made the following comments in reference to the question of dogmatism which he had to tackle within the Chinese Communist Party:
   > Both dogmatism and revisionism run counter to Marxism. Marxism must certainly advance; it must develop along with the development of practice and cannot stand still. It would become lifeless if it remained stagnant and stereotyped. However, the basic principles of Marxism must never be violated, or otherwise mistakes will be made. *It is dogmatism to approach Marxism from a metaphysical point of view and to regard it as something rigid.* It is revisionism to negate the basic principles of Marxism and to negate its universal truth. Revisionism is one form of bourgeois ideology. (My emphasis.)

   This passage is taken from *Quotations From Chairman Mao Tse-Tung* (Foreign Languages Press, Peking, 1967) p. 20.
97. Sweezy, P. M., "The Transition to Socialism", in Monthly Review, Vol. 23, No. 1, (May 1971) p. 7.
98. Lukács, G., op.cit., (see footnote 90 above) p. 24.
99. Ibid., op.cit., p. 31. It must be because Lloyd has failed to acquaint himself with what Marxism is saying about the question of class consciousness and class loyalties that he comes to write, rather superfluously, that, e.g., "Thus within a class will be those who continue to struggle to achieve their goals, those who seek alternative goals, and those who are apathetic. Furthermore, class consciousness implies cooperation to obtain shared goals and class ideology therefore has a strong egalitarian flavour; yet this is always countered by competition for power and rewards within the class and, perhaps, by the desire of some to move into the opposed class." (Op.cit., 1971, p. 17.)
100. Lloyd, P. C., op.cit., (1971) p. 76.
101. We regard the notion of "African socialism" as a myth used by the ruling classes to conceal the existence of relations of exploitation and class conflict in African societies. It is not accidental, therefore, that Lloyd accepts the application of this notion to African societies rather than that of class. He writes, for example, (op.cit., 1971, pp. 153—4):
   > Thus African leaders use the term socialist for their societies on the grounds that traditional communities were so structured; by extension, modern African society is also *socialist and classless.*
   > The term *socialist is also appropriate* in that it describes the existing high degree of state control of the economy, a heritage of the colonial situation in which the metropolitan power built the railways, and provided most of the services. (My emphasis.)
102. Lloyd, P. C., Africa in Social Change ..., op.cit., pp. 164 and 280.
   Cox, Idris, Socialist Ideas in Africa, (Lawrence and Wishart, London, 1966) p. 41.
103. Lloyd, P. C., op.cit., (1971) p. 76.

104. Bienen, Henry, *Tanzania: Party Transformation and Economic Development*, (Princeton University Press, 1970) p. 50. In this case the attempt to use tribalism to maintain a political position failed, as Bienen shows: "The British introduced and pressed their policy of multi-racialism, guaranteeing European and Asian minorities a political position which their numbers could not assure through the ballot. *They also tried unsuccessfully—to channel tribalism into sustaining the authority of the chiefs.*" (My emphasis.)

105. Mafeje, Archie, "The Ideology of 'Tribalism'", in *The Journal of Modern African Studies*, 9, 2 (1971) pp. 258—259.

Nkrumah, Kwame, *Class Struggle in Africa*, (International Publishers, New York, 1970). On page 59, Nkrumah makes the following comments on modern tribalism:

At Independence, the colonial powers again fostered separatism and tribal differences through the encouragement of federal constitutions. Genuine independence was prevented through the operation of diverse forms of neocolonialism. In the era of neocolonialism, tribalism is exploited by the bourgeois ruling classes as an instrument of power politics, and as useful outlet for the discontent of the masses. Many of the so-called tribal conflicts in modern Africa are in reality class forces brought into conflict by the transition from colonialism to neocolonialism. *Tribalism is the result, not the cause, of underdevelopment. In the majority of 'tribal' conflicts, the source is the exploiting bourgeois or feudal minority in cooperation with imperialists and neo-colonialists seeking to promote their joint class interests.* (My emphasis.)

It seems to me most puzzling, that the man who *never tires* of *beating on his tribal drum*; the man who attributes tribal sentiment and content to almost everything Africans say or do, seems utterly disinterested in the *racial sentiment*. Race and Racism, which are among the most important *components* of colonialism and imperialism, do not have a place in Peter Lloyd's writings on Africa and other parts of the former colonial territories. (See our further remarks on a similar point on page 99 above.)

106. Lloyd, P. C., Africa in Social Change . . ., op.cit., p. 295, of.cit. (1971) p. 144.

Smythe, H. H., and Smythe, M. M., *The New Nigerian Élites*, (Stanford University Press, California, 1960). On page 109, these authors comment:

Despite class feelings on the part of the élite, the popular notion that a Western education somehow separates an African irrevocably from his tribal identification was not borne out by the study. It is true that the educated élite live in Western houses, usually at some distance from their home villages, and they have forsaken long-revered superstitions and numerous other aspects of indigenous culture. It is also not true that their way of life is far different from that of the villagers. However, they did not consider these changes as removing the lasting appeal of allegiance to the tribe.

Stavenhagen, R., *Social Classes in Agrarian Societies*, op.cit. On page 34, Stavenhagen makes the following pertinent observation in regard to the meaning and use of social mobility:

We may go one step further and suggest that stratifications, as phenomena of the superstructure, and the product of certain class relations, react in turn upon these relations. They are not only a passive reflex. The middle strata of stratification systems tend to blunt the sharper oppositions that might exist between their two polarized extremes, when these extreme strata are at the same time social classes. *In 'open' systems of social stratification (i.e., where social mobility is possible), mobility performs the dual function of reducing the severity of opposition between classes while re-enforcing the stratification itself.* Thus it is clear that stratification is an essentially conservative device of social systems, whereas class oppositions and conflicts are basically dynamic. At the same time that social stratification divides society into groups, *it has the function of integrating society and consolidating given socio-economic structures.* (My emphasis.)

107. Lloyd, P. C., op.cit., (1971) p. 46.
108. Ibid., op.cit., p. 49.
   Rodney, W., op.cit., On page 236, Rodney has correctly asserted that "It is fairly obvious that capitalists do not set out to create other capitalists, who would be rivals. On the contrary, the tendency of capitalism in Europe from the very beginning was one of *competition, elimination and monopoly.* Therefore, when the imperialist stage was reached, the metropolitian capitalists *had no intention of allowing rivals to arise in the dependencies.*" (My epmhasis.)
109. Lloyd, P. C., op.cit., (1971) p. 61.
110. Ibid., op.cit., p. 52.
111. Ibid., op.cit., p. 9.
   Szentes, T., op.cit. On pages 12—13, Szentes issues a timely warning as to the confusions, and indeed, dangers, that might be involved in analysis in which class struggle comes to be seen as that existing between the poor and rich. He has commented:
   > An association of this conception with the vulgar—Marxist interpretation of class consciousness will, as a rule, result in the conclusion that the genuine revolutionary forces are represented by those having the lowest (money) income, and that the degree of poverty is proportional to that of revolutionarism. Projected, then, onto an international scale, this view will appear in the conception of confronting *the 'poor' countries with the 'rich'* ones as the front of the international 'class-struggle', which, despite all its 'anti-imperialist revolutionarism', tends to conceal the historical cause of 'poverty' and 'richness', the laws relating to the dynamics of capitalist world economy, and the role of colonialism. (Emphasis in the original.)
112 Buchanan, Keith, *The Geography of Empire,* (Spokesman Books, The Russell Press, 1972) p. 14. On page 15, Buchanan makes the following observations:
   > This 'aid' is very sensitive to internal conditions; thus 'aid' to Colombia reached a peak ($1.8 million) in 1966, the year Camilo Torres was killed, while 'aid' to the Philippines has climbed steadily as internal tensions have increased in recent years. By contrast, countries like Liberia or Venezuela, in which repression has become endemic, show a more steady year to year level of American help in keeping the disaffected 'in their place'.
113. Lloyd, P. C. These claims are made in almost all this writings on Africa.
114. Armed struggles in the Portuguese colonies of Guinea, Mozambique and Angola, as well as in Rhodesia, started at the end of the 1950's-beginning of the 1960's. And, as it is well-known, the vast majority of the population in all the three former Portuguese colonies are composed of peasants who can neither read nor write. Some basic information and facts about these struggles for national liberation will be found in the following books, out of a vast literature available:
   Cabral, Amilcar, *Revolution in Guinea: An African People's Struggle, Stage 1,* op.cit.; *Return to the Source: Selected Speeches of Amilcar Cabral,* edited by African Information Service (Monthly Review Press, 1973).
   Davidson, Basil, *The Liberation of Guiné: Aspects of an African Revolution,* (Penguin Books, 1969).
   Davidson, Basil, *In the Eye of the Storm: Angola's People,* (Penguin Books, 1974).
   Mondlane, Eduardo, *The Struggle for Mozambique,* (Penguin Books, 1969).
   Soul, John, "Frelimo and the Mozambique Revolution", in *Monthly Review, No. 10,* (March, 1973) pp. 23—51. The same issue contains an article on Guiné by Charles McCollester.
   "Frelimo Faces the Future", Marcelino Dos Santos, Vice-President of Frelimo, in-

terviewed by Joe Slovo in *The African Communist, No. 55*, 1973, pp. 23—53.
Machel, Samora, *Sowing the Seeds of Revolution*, (London, Committee for Freedom in Mozambique, Angola and Guiné, 1974).

115. Lloyd, P. C., op.cit., see pages 76—78 above.
116. Frelimo (Front for the Liberation of Mozambique), and PAIGC (African Independence Party of Guiné and the Cape Verde Islands), as well as their social and political programmes are described and analysed in the literature listed under footnote 114 above, and footnote 117 below.
117. Rudebeck, Lars, *Guinea-Bissau: A Study of Political Mobilization*, (The Scandinavian Institute of African Studies, Uppsala, 1974).
118. Ibid., op.cit., p. 238.
119. Ibid., op.cit., p. 244.
120. Ibid., op.cit., p. 230. In the case of Guinea-Bissau, the process of mobilization was directed against Portuguese colonialism, and in this particular situation, mobilization
... has meant convincing a peasant population, often reluctant and superstitious, of the necessity to fight a war of national liberation in order to meet their most elementary needs for material satisfaction and life in peace and human dignity. By this very fact, the organizers of rebellion and revolution in Guinea-Bissau have also been forced to sustain popular support by daily *demonstration in practice of the credibility of the PAIGC alternative to the colonial system*. Had they failed in this demonstration, the support would no longer have been forthcoming, and a successful people's war would have been impossible, pp. 230—231. (My emphasis.)
121. Deutch, Karl, W., "Social Mobilization and Political Development", in *The American Political Science Review, Vol. LV, September, 1961, No. 3*. In this article in which social mobilization is viewed as "an overall process of change, which happens to substantial parts of the population in countries which are moving from traditional to modern ways of life", Deutch fails to deal with the crucial question of how this all happens. He sees the process, therefore, almost completely as something that happens spontaneously, and it has to do largely with moving from "tradition" to "modernity". In fact, Deutch does raise the question, "how?", but he quickly pushes it aside by suggesting that "how" must be supplemented with "how much?", (p. 493). This leads to a preoccupation with measurements, in which Deutch becomes engrossed with the formulation of abstract indices and indicators of social mobilization or modernization. These are the indices whose refinement are seen to be the main task of modernization theory in years to come, according to Eisenstadt, (see page 29 above).
Rudebeck has criticised this conception of mobilization in more detail. He has also criticized some Marxist writers such as Samir Amin and Gunder Frank, for tendencies "to de-emphasize the importance of studying in detail the *conditions and mechanisms of internal mobilization against*" the relationships of exploitation and domination which they otherwise describe and analyse so well, (p. 239). (My emphasis.)
122. For a very instructive description and analysis of the emergence, development and maturation of a political movement from a purely nationalist to one of the most revolutionary liberation movements in Africa, we recommend the interview cited above in *The African Communist* (footnote 114).
The definition and redefinition of some of the central questions will always include, in the case of African liberation struggles against colonialism, the crucial distinction that must be made between *imperialism in the form of colonialism*, on the one hand, and *racism, racial discrimination or apartheid*, on the other. Success or failure to clearly draw this distinction on the part of the leadership is one of the more accurate indicators of whether the particular leadership is purely *nationalist/petty bourgeois*,

whose objectives in the struggle are confined to limited and superficial reforms, or *revolutionary*, in which case Independence day only marks an important stage in the course of a long class struggle that will and must continue. In terms of mobilization, the former engages in limited and "fictitious" social mobilization aimed at the ousting of the White colonial ruling class in order to replace it with a Black one, and henceforth "mobilization" takes place only at intervals when the "élites compete for the vote of the electorate".

123. Outside the African experience, the most illuminating *lessons* on social and political mobilization, during and after the struggle for national independence, *can be learned* from the revolutionary experience of the People's Republic of China. This subject is more than well covered in the following few titles:

Snow, Edgar, *Red Star Over China* (Penguin Books, revised edition, 1968); and *Red China Today: The Other Side of the River* (Penguin Books edition, 1970).

Schurmann, Franz, *Ideology and Organization in Communist China*, op.cit.

Bettelheim, Charles, *Cultural Revolution and Industrial Organization in China: Changes in Management and the Division of Labour* (Monthly Review Press, 1974).

Wheelright, E. L., and McFarlane, B., *The Chinese Road To Socialism* (Monthly Review Press, 1971).

Bibliography

African Experiment in Radio Forums for Rural Development: Ghana, 1964—65, (Unesco).

Apter, D., *The Politics of Modernization,* (University of Chicago Press, 1965).

Ayandele, E. A., *The Educated Élite in the Nigerian Society,* (Ibadan University Press, 1974).

Balandier, Georges, *Political Anthropology,* (Penguin Books edition, 1970).

Batten, T. R., *The Human Factor in Community Work,* (Oxford University Press, 1965).

Batten, T. R., *Training for Community Development: A Critical Study of Method,* (Oxford University Press, 1962).

Berger, P. L., and Luckmann, T., *The Social Construction of Reality: A Treatise in the Sociology of Knowledge,* (Anchor Books Edition, 1967).

Brembeck, Cole S., Hovey, Richard L., *Educational Programmes in Rural Areas,* (Paris, Unesco, 1972).

Buitron, Anibal, *Community Development in Latin America: A Practical Guide to Community Development Workers,* (East African Literature Bureau, Nairobi, 1966).

Coates, K. and Silburn, R., *Poverty: The Forgotten Englishmen,* (Penguin Books, 1970).

Community Work and Social Change: A Report on Training, (The Calouste Gulbenkian Foundation), (Longman Group Ltd., 1968).

Cornforth, Maurice, *Dialectical Materialism: An Introduction, Vols. I—III,* (Lawrence and Wishart, London, 1952).

Crook, David and Isabel, *Revolution in a Chinese Village: Ten Mile Inn,* (Routledge and Kegan Paul, 1959).

Djilas, Milovan, *The New Class: An Analysis of the Communist System,* (George Allen and Unwin, London, 1957).

Dube, C. S., *India's Changing Villages,* (Routledge and Kegan Paul, 1958).

Eisenstadt, S. N., "Primitive Political Systems: A Preliminary Comparative Analysis", in *American Anthropology, Vol. 61,* 1959.

Freire, Paulo, *Pedagogy of the Oppressed,* (Penguin Books Edition, 1972).

Gluckman, M., *Politics, Law and Ritual in Tribal Society,* (Clarendon Press, London, 1965).

Hale, S. M., "Barriers to Free Choice in Development", in *Community Development: International Issue of 'Centro Sociale', New Series 33.34.,* August 1975.

Hamilton, William, editor, *Transfer of Institutions,* (Duke University Press, Durham, N.C., 1964).

Harrington, Michael, *The Other America: Poverty in the United States,* (Penguin Books, Baltimore, Maryland, 1962).

Harris, F. J., *Social Casework: An Introduction For Students in Developing Countries,* (Oxford University Press, Nairobi, 1970).

Haroub, Othman, "The Tanzanian State", *in Monthly Review, Vol. 26, No. 7,* (December 1974).

Higgs, John, *People in the Countryside: Studies in Rural Social Development,* (London, 1966).

Himmelstrand, U., and Rudquist, A., "Structural Contradictions, Predicaments and Social Change. Some Theoretical and Empirical Observations", in *Community Develop-*

ment: *International Issue of "Centro Sociales", New Series 33.34.*, August 1975, pp. 1—22.

Hodgkin, Thomas, "The Vietnamese Revolution and Some Lessons", in *Race and Class, Vol. XVI, January, 1975, No. 3*, pp. 233—249.

Horowitz, David, "Alliance For Progress", in *The Socialist Register*, (Merlin Press, 1964) pp. 127—145.

Horowitz, David, editor, *Containment and Revolution: Western Policy Towards Social Revolution 1917 to Vietnam*, (Anthony Blond Ltd., 1967).

"Imperialism and People's War", in *Review of African Political Economy, Number 4*, November 1975, by the editors.

Kincaid, J. C., *Poverty and Equality in Britain: A Study of Social Security and Taxation*, (Penguin Books, 1973).

Lamb, Geoff, *Peasant Politics*, (Julian Friedmann Publishers Ltd., 1974).

Leonard, Peter, *Sociology in Social Work*, (Routledge and Kegan Paul, 1966).

Livingstone, Arthur, *Social Policy in Developing Countries*, (Routledge and Kegan Paul, 1969).

Mao, Tse-tung, Selected Military Writings, (Foreign Languages Press, Peking, 1968).

Meisel, J. H., editor, *Pareto and Mosca*, (Englewood Cliffs, N.J., 1965).

Mészáros, I., *The Necessity of Social Control*, (The Merlin Press, London, 1971).

Mezirow, J. D., *Dynamics of Community Development*, (Scarecrow Press, New York, 1963).

Miliband, Ralph, *State in Capitalist Society: The Analysis of the Western System of Power*, (Quartet Books, London, 1969).

Mills, C. Wright, *The Marxists*, (Dell Publishing Co., Inc., NY, 1962).

Mosca, Gaetano, *The Ruling Class*, (New York, 1939).

Narain, B., "Health Programmes in Community Project Areas", in *The Indian Journal of Public Administration, 1*, 1955).

Nguyen Khac Vien, *Tradition and Revolution in Vietnam*, edited by David Marr and Jayne Werner, (Indo-China Resource Center, Berkely and Washington, 1974).

O'Brien, Donald, B. C., *Saints and Politicians: Essays in the Organization of a Senegalese Peasant Society*, (Cambridge University Press, 1975).

Ossowski, Stanislaw, *Class Structure in the Social Consciousness*, (New York, 1963).

Post, K. W. J., and Vickers, M., *Structure and Conflict in Nigeria, 1960—1965*, (Heineman Edulational Books Ltd., 1973).

Ross, Murray, *Community Organization: Theory and Practice*, (Harper and Brothers, New York, 1955).

Saul, John, "Free Mozambique", in *Monthly Review, Volume 27, No. 7*, December 1975, pp. 8—22.

Schmidt, Alfred, *The Concept of Nature in Marx*, (New Left Books, 1971).

Shivji, Issa, "Peasants and Class Alliances", in *Review of African Political Economy, Number 3*, May—October 1975, pp. 10—18.

Smith, Stewart, *U.S. Neocolonialism in Africa*, (International Publishers, NY, 1974).

Villaneuva, B. M., "Administrative Aspects of Community Development", (UN Seminar, The Hague, 1959).

Vincent, Joan, *African Élite: The Big Men of a Small Town*, (Columbia University Press, 1971).

De Vries, E., "Community Development and Development", in *International Review of Community Development, No. 5*, 1960, pp. 87—94.

Wolfers, Michael, *Black Man's Burden Revisited*, (Allison and Busby, London, 1974).

Zwanikken, W. A. C., "Community Development in the Netherlands", in *The Community Development Journal, Vol. 3*, 1968, pp. 143—151.

~ Next thurs. Lecture RAT
d
Giddens

~ Following wed. ?